JAMES C. SCHAAP

SOMEONE'S SINGING, LORD

DEVOTIONS ▾ FOR TODAY'S FAMILY

CRCPUBLICATIONS
Grand Rapids, Michigan

To Friend
D1ɛt.
love.
James C.
Schaap

Copyright © 1989 CRC Publications, 2850 Kalamazoo SE,
Grand Rapids, Michigan 49560

Library of Congress Cataloging-in-Publication Data
Schaap, James., 1948-
Someone's Singing, Lord / James C. Schaap.
p. cm. — (Devotions of today's family)
ISBN 0-930265-79-3
1. Family—Prayer-books and devotions–English. I. Title.
II. Series.
BV255.S22 1989
249—dc20   89-39654
CIP

5 4 3 2 1

CONTENTS

Preface 7

AMAZING GRACE
Meditations 1-5 10

GOD MOVES IN A MYSTERIOUS WAY
Meditations 6-10 22

NOW THANK WE ALL OUR GOD
Meditations 11-16 34

GUIDE ME, O MY GREAT REDEEMER
Meditations 17-21 48

LEAD ON, O KING ETERNAL
Meditations 22-26 60

JESUS SHALL REIGN WHERE'ER THE SUN
Meditations 27-31 72

OH, FOR A THOUSAND TONGUES TO SING
Meditations 32-36 84

ABIDE WITH ME
Meditations 37-40 96

PREFACE

At a time when in many parts of the world the family seems to be in crisis, torn apart by social and economic changes, family devotions have growing importance. Pausing for worship together—before or after meals, or before bedtime—may be a critical element in preserving family faith.

Bible reading and prayer are the usual components of such devotions. But many families appreciate some additional guide to structure their Bible reading and spark discussions about the Christian faith and life. With small children, parents often use a Bible storybook. But for families who have older children or children of a wide range of ages, finding appropriate material that appeals to all is more difficult.

Devotions for Today's Family is a series of family devotional booklets written at a middle-school reading level. Each devotion suggests a Scripture reading and offers a prayer. Between these it either tells a story—a story that reflects on the week's theme and the day's Scripture, a story that flows out of the Christian life, a story that challenges family members to think and talk about their faith—or it reflects on something in the theme or Scripture in a personal and vivid way that makes the ideas come alive. These stories and reflections speak to boys and girls, to children and adults, to young and old. They are ageless.

Someone's Singing, Lord is the title of this devotional booklet. Eight well-known, often-sung, and deeply loved songs, such as "Amazing Grace" and "Abide with Me," provide the themes for Scripture, meditation, and prayer. These familiar words of faith, written by the hymn writers in earlier generations, take on new meaning and poignancy through the modern stories and meditations the author has written about them.

James C. Schaap, author of *Someone's Singing, Lord*, is a professor of English at Dordt College in Sioux Center, Iowa. Prolific writer of short stories and authentic reflector of the Reformed ethos in a Midwest context, James Schaap is above all a Christian who thinks deeply and writes wisely about his own faith experience. His published works include *CRC Family Portrait* and *Intermission*, a popular book of devotionals for teenagers.

Someone's Singing, Lord is offered with the prayer that it may help your family find a greater unity and a greater depth of faith and life.

Harvey A. Smit
Editor in Chief
Education Department
CRC Publications

AMAZING GRACE

1 A - maz - ing grace— how sweet the sound—
2 'Twas grace that taught my heart to fear,
3 The Lord has prom - ised good to me,
4 Through man - y dan - gers, toils, and snares
5 When we've been there ten thou - sand years,

that saved a wretch like me! I once was lost
and grace my fears re - lieved; how pre - cious did
► his word my hope se - cures; he will my shield
I have al - read - y come; 'tis grace hath brought
bright shin - ing as the sun, we've no less days

but now am found, was blind but now I see.
that grace ap - pear the hour I first be - lieved!
► and por - tion be as long as life en - dures.
me safe thus far, and grace will lead me home.
to sing God's praise than when we'd first be - gun.

Text: st. 1–4, John Newton, 1779; st. 5, A Collection of Sacred Ballads, 1790
Tune: Virginia Harmony, 1831; adapt. and harm. Edwin O. Excell, 1900

CM
NEW BRITAIN

SALVATION AT SEA

....

Ephesians 2:1-9

I'm a born-and-reared midwesterner, so I'd never jiggled through an earthquake until just a few weeks ago. When it started, I thought some fat man was stomping around behind me. In fact, I turned around to see who it was. Not until I noticed that the chandelier was swaying was I convinced that we were being tumbled around by an authentic California earthquake.

Although I'm no daredevil, the quake didn't scare me much. I thought it was kind of fun. But my daughter and my wife got shook up about it (that's a bad pun, I know). And all of us admitted that while the room was shaking, we felt *powerless*.

I grew up with tornadoes. Californians sweat bullets when they imagine tornadoes. But lots of midwesterners have seen tornadoes; some claim they can smell them.

But no one can sniff out earthquakes. This one came at noon on a day of glorious California sunshine. Suddenly the earth began to jiggle and roll. We could do nothing, run nowhere. Rumble, rumble—and we were powerless.

That kind of powerlessness plays a role in the story of the famous hymn "Amazing Grace." Its writer, John Newton, hung on to his ship for dear life one night during a titanic ocean storm. He felt as powerless as Californians do during an earthquake.

In many ways a storm on water is like an earthquake. When it comes, you simply have to ride it out. Everything shakes and rattles and sways; the ship lurches in the swelling waves, and there's nowhere to hide.

Newton said he thought of himself as Jonah. He thought the whole ship was going down because of his sins. You see, John Newton had done a lot of ugly things—much uglier than stealing cigarettes or spitting out a naughty word.

In fact, Newton sat like the prodigal son in the dirtiest sins of his time. He was a slave trader. He dealt in human souls as if people were pigs. The ships he captained jammed hundreds of African blacks, people ripped away from families and homes, into the pitch darkness of the hold. Once he got them into port, he sold them—he sold human flesh.

Newton was an evil man. They don't come much worse.

But one night in the middle of a storm, John Newton, English slaver, felt totally powerless. And in that powerlessness, he groped around in the darkness of his own life and found nothing at all could save his worthless skin and soul but God Almighty.

Like Jonah the prodigal, Newton had tried to run away and be bad. But God found Newton on the high seas. "I once was lost but now am found" is the testimony of a lost man who knew evil inside and out, a man who'd bathed in sin. But God himself picked John Newton out of the hold of evil and brought him into the light.

And it changed him forever. Newton gave up the slave trade and spent the rest of his days on earth telling people about Christ's gift of love.

That's John Newton's powerful story of truly amazing grace.

Dear Lord, thank you for saving us, even those of us whose lives are marked with sins that make headlines. Your forgiveness is the finest, deepest cleaning we will ever know. It brings us to glory in you.
Thank you. Amen.

THE GIFT OF GRACE

....

Ephesians 1:1-7

Picture this.

You get home late. You've been at a party or a music concert or a late ball game, and you're dead tired. You haven't done a stitch of homework, and you know you could get nailed the next day if you don't. But your father says to put out the light—it's already past eleven. Okay, you figure; it says somewhere to obey your parents. The light goes out. Your history book sits in the knapsack, your notes still stuck inside.

The next day your history teacher, Mr. Barands, decides to give a surprise quiz on those notes. Franco-Prussian War, Stonewall Jackson, 1066, Ho Chi Minh, Trotsky, the Parthenon—no matter what he asks on his disgusting quiz, you know your goose is cooked. Just when you were scrambling for a B.

"Okay, hand them up," he says, cheerfully, as if the day is soaked in sunshine. You feel sick—like the time your new T-shirt shrunk so much you had to give it to your sister.

Barands is no monster. In fact, he's bald and kind of crazy, and almost everyone likes him. You figure that maybe if you get down on your knees and beg him after school, plead with him about how your own father told you you couldn't study—tell him everything, slobber all over, kiss his thick-soled shoes—maybe he'll let you off.

Then Barands does this whacky thing that nobody expects. He grabs the bunch of quizzes—including your zero—in his fist, stares at them for a minute, then rips up the whole stack, as if he were some iron-pumper trying to wow the class.

"This time I'll give you a break," he says. "I don't have time to correct them tonight anyway. But next time—"

Your stomach flattens, squeaky noises emerge involuntarily from your throat, and your eyes widen. You're free. You were all ready to kiss off history, and just like that, with a few choice words, Barands blew your headache right out the door. What Barands did by ripping up the papers is something like what this song is about—something like grace.

Grace is forgiveness. It happens when God, completely on his own, decides to throw away our bad days without holding them against us. It happens when he snatches the darkness away and makes the whole world glow, with him at the very center.

Grace is Christ, our gift from God—someone who gave us life with his death when we really didn't deserve it. Grace is life in Christ. A miracle.

The incredible thing is that grace is free. We don't deserve it or earn it. He gives it to us—"Here, take my forgiveness, feel my joy," he says. "If it was good enough to save a slave hunter like John Newton, it'll do for you. What's more," he says, "there'll be no charge."

That's amazing grace. It's free. Picture that.

It amazes us, Lord, that your grace is free. You give us life for no real reason other than your love for us. Because you loved us, you sent your Son. Thank you, Lord. Amen.

RICH AND WRETCH

....

1 John 1

A whopping 95 percent of the American people consider themselves "middle class." Some people consider themselves poor, some consider themselves richest of the rich; but those "somes," in sum, make up only 5 percent of the population.

What that means is that lots of folks are deceiving themselves. The middle class doesn't stretch to 95 percent of the American people. Someone's foggy somewhere, and it's easy to see why.

After all, how many of you consider yourselves "upper class"? Don't all speak at once. How many of you are really rich? Get your hands up there. I can't see them.

As long as Lee Iococca hauls in a couple-dozen million in salary; as long as Mike Tyson gets twenty million for taking some thug to the mat in a minute and a half; as long as DuPonts live in Palm Beach, none of us poor folk will ever really consider ourselves rich.

But if we forget about the Iococcas and the DuPonts and compare ourselves to some starving Ethiopians, everything changes. Next to many Ethiopians, we live like royalty.

Being rich is relative. It's like being wretched. To us, some people are always richer, just as some people are always uglier, more despicable, more ornery, and plain old wicked.

Dirty old John Newton would have made a junkyard dog look like Mother Theresa. We've already run through a roster of his sins. He made big bucks selling human beings. He lived like an outlaw. In fact, he *was* an outlaw. He cared about nothing but his own stuffed pockets. So when John Newton sang his own song, he was right in calling himself a wretch.

But not me. After all, in the last two months I've daringly steered a half-dozen old folks across intersections swarming with New York cab drivers. I'm a good guy. I'm no wretch. I never sold slaves. I don't beat my wife. I don't lie around dead drunk. Hey, I go to church!—I'm no wretch.

Maybe so.

It's likely that no one reading this book was ever really rotten, hellish, or perverse. We're all pretty decent folks, if you ask us. Good people. Maybe a naughty word now and then, but nothing really satanic, nothing big-time.

So maybe when we sing "Amazing Grace," we should think of John Newton, the slave dealer. He was wretched. We aren't.

Baloney.

"If we claim we are without sin, we are liars," John tells us in his first epistle. "The truth is not in us." Our own sin is as hard for us to recognize as our wealth. Yet, John says, all of us—every single man, woman, and child—stand in need of Newton's own brand of amazing grace.

There may be no warmongers, no child molesters, no prostitutes, no mass murderers in your house, but all of us—me, and you too—need God's gift of grace, because without it we're all (gulp!) wretched.

Put it this way: to know that I'm a wretch is to know I need God and his Son's saving grace. That's rich.

....

We need you, Lord. Sometimes we have trouble admitting it because we think we're pretty good. But we know that without you we can't find joy or happiness. Thank you for your amazing grace. Amen.

MARNEE'S HOME (1)

....

Romans 5:1-5

Marnee had expected *Sherry* to fall apart at the airport— they were best buddies, after all. But Sherry's mom got all teary too. Even her little brother Tim had to turn away when Marnee walked down through the gate. They had all cried.

As the plane took off, Marnee was still wiping tears from her face. She had only flown once before, so she wanted to catch every word of the flight attendant's little lecture. As she listened, she thought about the last time she had traveled in an airplane—the week her father had taken them to Arizona to try to sell them on moving.

That all seemed like ancient history now. Marnee's family had already moved to the big, hot city filled with palm trees and cactuses— cacti, she remembered, not cactuses.

Marnee had never wanted to move; she was the oldest, the only one who was already in high school. She was also the only catcher on her softball team. Marnee's parents had made a deal with her: if she'd stop complaining about the move, they'd let her spend one last summer with her old friends, one last summer playing star catcher for her ball team. She'd accepted the deal and spent the summer with Sherry's family.

"You're all by yourself?" the guy sitting next to her asked, once they had been in the air for awhile.

She didn't look into his eyes. She was stuck in the middle between a guy in suspenders—a college guy maybe, maybe older—and a rich guy with sideburns. Elbow to elbow. Jam-packed. It was the one in suspenders who had spoken.

"My parents are picking me up in Arizona," she said.

His legs were crossed so that his shoe stuck out into the aisle. He had an open *Sports Illustrated* draped over his knee. She thought that if he liked sports, he couldn't be all bad.

"You live there?" he asked.

"We just moved," she told him.

"Rough," he said. "It's tough stuff to move."

Everyone heard the explosion. Even though she couldn't see the wing, Marnee heard people talking about an engine in flames. The whole plane tipped, and the jet fell as if a huge hand had suddenly let it drop. It swooped sideways, so that Marnee had to look down to see out the window, then righted itself again.

"What's going—" Marnee tried to get something out, but the whole cabin twisted sharply again to the right and the guy's magazine flew past her toward the man at the window. That's when the warning lights flashed and the flight attendant fought her way to the mike. Her voice stuttered out something about "going to land," but her face was painted in horror.

Marnee's first thought, her very first, in those fractured seconds, was that she'd never wanted to move in the first place and that, if she died, she'd get her wish. She could just see her father at the airport, all twisted in grief. They should never have moved. Her death would prove it.

And that's when she knew she was going to die. Her mind raced through everything that would happen, the plane spinning down and crashing, the bodies in the morgue, the funeral, her parents' grief—as if all of it were on film.

She was going to die. For the first time in her life she knew she was going to die. She wanted it to happen quickly. That's what she asked the Lord. Don't let there be pain.

That was the first of Marnee's prayers.

Father, we know that each second, each minute, each hour of our lives is in your hands. Relieve our fears and help us to rest in the peace of knowing you are Ruler over all that happens—you are Lord of the universe. Amen.

RIDDLE ME THIS—

....
Psalm 86:11-13

Here's a riddle for you: "What's the difference between the Lincoln Tunnel and a crazy Dutchman?"

(Go ahead, gnaw on that for awhile. It's not too tough.) Give up? Okay, here's the answer (please, no heavy groaning). One is a hollow cylinder and the other a silly Hollander. (My son will call that sick.)

Okay, try this one on for size: Which Old Testament character had the sharpest business mind?

(Hey, don't read the answer right away. Think about it.)

Give up? I knew you would. Okay, you pinheads, the answer is Moses' sister Miriam. Why? She did the impossible. She drew a "prophet" from a "rush" on the "bank." Got you there.

Riddles, really, are nothing more than word games—clever nonsense. They can be really ridiculous:

Q. What purple military genius conquered the world?

A. Alexander the Grape;

Or, they can be deep and poetic, like the riddles in *The Hobbit:*

This thing all things devours:

Birds, beasts, trees, flowers;

Gnaws iron, bites steel;

Slays king, ruins town,

And beats high mountain down.

The answer, as Bilbo Baggins discovers almost accidentally, is *time.* (You may want to zip through that again.)

Stanza five of "Amazing Grace" is really a species of riddle. That's what makes it hard to understand the first time through. It's not particularly silly or weird; it's merely a fresh way of saying something that's been said before.

When we've been there ten thousand years,
bright shining as the sun,
we've no less days to sing God's praise
than when we'd first begun.

There, in the first line, the author (not Newton—this stanza was added eleven years later) refers to the word *home* in the last line of the fourth verse: "grace will lead me home." Paraphrased, the verse might read as follows:

When we've been with God in glory,
shining in his light for ten thousand long years,
we'll still have all of forever to praise him.

So the verse is a kind of riddle—not one that begs for a tricky answer but simply a way of describing eternity. The author found a subtle way to emphasize Newton's point: the amazing grace that saved wretches like us will make us all glow in glory forever and forever—as if ten thousand years (our time) were nothing but a camera flash. Ten thousand years down here on earth's sidewalks—3,650,000 days—is "poof" in heaven.

The rewards of grace are that immense, says the stanza, echoing the thoughts of the man who used to steal people from their homes and sell them. Not only is my sin forgiven, but I'll live forever in God's joy.

Grace, says the wretch, is that incredible. Amazing—grace.

Forever is a long time, Lord. We can't even imagine a world without time. Yet we know that your grace saves us forever, for eternity. Help us keep eternity in mind when it seems that time is so precious. Remind us that we have life forever in you. In your Son's name, Amen.

GOD MOVES IN A MYSTERIOUS WAY

1 God moves in a mys-te-rious way his won-ders to per-form.
2 Deep in un-fath-om-a-ble mines of nev-er-fail-ing skill,
3 You fear-ful saints, fresh cour-age take; the clouds you so much dread
4 His pur-pos-es will rip-en fast, un-fold-ing ev-ery hour.
5 Blind un-be-lief is sure to err and scan his work in vain.

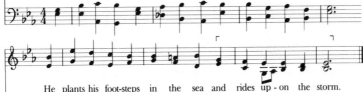

He plants his foot-steps in the sea and rides up-on the storm.
he trea-sures up his bright de-signs and works his sov-ereign will.
are big with mer-cy and shall break in bless-ings on your head.
The bud may have a bit-ter taste, but sweet will be the flower.
God is his own in-ter-pret-er, and he will make it plain.

Text: William Cowper, 1774
Tune: Scottish Psalter, 1615; harm. Thomas Ravenscroft, c. 1592–1635, alt.

CM
DUNDEE

OF MYSTERIOUS WAYS

....
Psalm 107:23-31

I'm about to tell you a story about the origin of "God Moves in a Mysterious Way." Some historians claim this story is true; others say it's pure fiction.

The fact is, the man who wrote this song, William Cowper, a well-known English poet, didn't always know up from down. He was at times, as we used to say, a little bit "off." And he spent considerable chunks of his life planning suicide.

But this is the story. . . .

On one of the really dark nights of his life, Cowper asked the driver of his team to take him to the river. The driver slapped his reins against the horses' flanks, and they were off. This was no ordinary drive to the river. The darkness sat between the seats like a heavy wall, and Cowper's thoughts were even darker. He told his driver that the Lord had spoken to him—the Lord had told him he was damned and should, therefore, kill himself. That's why they were headed for the river: Cowper had chosen drowning over hanging or shooting.

My guess is that right about then the driver started grinding his teeth. He couldn't, he knew, simply deliver a man to his own watery death. So as the fog circled the treetops, then descended in a heavy veil, the driver began (accidentally on purpose) to get himself quite effectively "lost" in the woods. Time passed. Cowper, it is said, eventually fell asleep.

After a couple hours of sifting through the inky silence of a night bound in mist, the driver turned his team back toward Cowper's place and, once there, woke the sleeping poet.

"Where are we?" Cowper said, rubbing his eyes.

"Why, sir—we're back at your home. I lost my way in the fog," said the driver—something of a sugar-coated lie.

Cowper, who was, as you remember, a little shaky, jumped immediately to the conclusion that God himself had decided not to let him take his own life. Instead, he had turned things around completely, and in the process, chosen Cowper for life.

The story goes that the poet, that very night, sat at his desk with a quill and penned the words of this well-known hymn. Cowper spent most of his later years in nearly perpetual horror, absolutely confident he was specially appointed by God Almighty to be damned in hell. That obsession didn't make him the life of the party.

And yet, this hymn has been a favorite of God's people for almost two hundred years. The man haunted by fiery visions of himself tortured in hell created stanzas that have brought joy and peace and confidence to thousands of believers.

Put it this way. The man who created the comfort in the song felt barely a dime's worth in his own soul in those later years. What he gave to thousands, he could himself never receive.

Cowper's story is proof of the song's message: God sometimes works in very mysterious ways.

....

Dear Lord, thank you for this song, for the comfort it has brought to many people for so long. Thank you for Mr. Cowper, who wrote it, too. Thank you for all of those who bring praise to your name through music. Amen.

STAR WARS

....
Psalm 18:4-17

A year before my son ever saw a *Star Wars* movie, he could pick out Hans Solo's picture in any toy store. In fact, before he or any of his friends had heard Darth Vader's breath wheeze through his helmet, they had spent hours dueling with fake lazer swords.

Hollywood saw what kind of affect Stephen Spielberg had on kids and carted his idea to the nearest Xerox machine. Today, even though the *Star Wars* movies themselves are history, there's always a fantasy thriller playing somewhere in the neighborhood, some show featuring warty ogres or cuddly ET's or fleets of space ships blowing up like cosmic bottle rockets.

William Cowper creates a kind of *Star Wars* Jehovah in the first verse of his famous hymn: "He plants his footsteps in the sea,/and rides upon the storm." In addition to suggesting Christ's own walk on the water before his astonished disciples, this line creates a Spielberg image of the Father and Creator of the universe. Someone simply awesome.

God the Father has given us a God to see in his Son, Jesus. But it's always been hard to imagine what kind of shape God the Father must have—if he has a shape at all.

How do you draw a being who sees every silly sparrow in every single garage in the world—and knows when they fall? How do you picture a God who counts hairs on the heads of millions of people? What does a God look like who can simultaneously nestle himself into the hearts of every single believer on this planet?

We could make up a list of "un-words": unapproachable, unknowable, uncreated. But we can't see a picture in any of those words.

What is he, really? Is *he* even the right word? In Psalm 18, David tries to put down in earth-shaking detail what he saw and felt when God's hand swept him away from death. Picture this passage like a movie:

First, a booming earthquake shakes the theater, and the screen dissolves behind thick smoke pumped out in huge jets. Then the light rises and the camera pans through the haze to roaring flames. The angry sky cracks wide open and God himself, wrapped in night's blackness and surrounded by a storm, breaks loose in a triumphant quest for the one who has begged for deliverance. Before him, rains fall in arrows and lightning slashes to the earth. Thunder crackles, then roars like a thousand rumbling engines as the earth turns itself inside out, mighty rivers emptying themselves, mountains crumbling.

What a great intro! David's picture would make Spielberg clammy. Any God who plants his footsteps in the sea and rides upon the storm is a God of immense power and life—an eternal God who burns through the limits of time and place as if they were little more than crinkly old film.

Even his shape is mystery. This is God, the great I AM, the one who gives life and breath to the entire universe.

And what's most astounding, what's enough to take my breath away, is that this incredible, awesome God loves us.

Wow!—and Amen.

*Dear Father, we are awed by your mystery, overwhelmed by your greatness and power. We praise you for creating us and for being concerned about the details of our lives. We praise you for your love.
Amen.*

STRANGE, VERY STRANGE

....
Romans 11:33-36

Christians aren't supposed to laugh about people—especially people with problems. But just this once it's okay to chuckle.

A man named Dennis Genz ate too much too often. In fact, he ate so much that he almost gobbled himself to death. Today's news didn't exactly say what Mr. Genz ate, but why don't we just picture him with a six-pack of chocolate malts. After all, a guy doesn't zoom up to 433 pounds on red cabbage and bean sprouts.

Apparently Mr. Genz had no medical problems that caused his obesity. That makes it easier to laugh. Obesity was a problem for him, but not something he couldn't help. He simply inhaled food until the time came when he couldn't find a chair big enough to sit in.

Gluttony is, as you know, a sin. Centuries ago, when monks used to chart the types of sins people could commit, they claimed that gluttony came in seventh—after pride, envy, wrath, sloth (laziness), lust, and avarice (greed).

But I'm off the subject. Mr. Dennis Genz, at 433 pounds of paunch, had to lose weight. He must have set his mind to it, because today he weighs in at a svelte 260. That's right—173 pounds of ugly flesh gone, vanished.

Well, not quite vanished. When what was a 433-pound man sheds almost one-third of his bulk, he doesn't turn magically into a well-pumped Hulk Hogan.

Think of it this way. A few months ago my daughter had a party in our basement, where I'm sitting right now. She hung streamers and balloons from the ceiling. Since I'm the one who spends the most time in the basement, it's my job to keep it clean. And I know I should have picked up the balloons long ago. But I didn't. I will, I swear, as soon as I'm done with this.

You know what two-month-old balloons look like? They've shrunk into pudgy, mushroom-like ugliness.

With its stuffing removed, a fat body looks about the same. You've heard of a double chin? When Mr. Genz lost all that weight, he found himself with a quadruple belly. So he had an operation to get all that excess flab removed.

I'm really sorry for being so indelicate, but hang in there. Dennis Genz comes out of this a hero.

You see, he gave all of that flab to the University of Chicago Medical Center. What on earth for? All that two-month-old-balloon-like skin is immensely valuable—even if it is gross.

Four feet square of skin may not be enough for a pup tent, but it is enough to provide temporary skin for dozens of people with severe burns. In fact, already yesterday a little boy named Dexter, badly burned in a house fire, used some of Mr. Genz's skin.

Who would have believed that all that horrible, rippling excess fat could be worth anything? You can hardly discuss it decently. But four square feet of flab is a bonanza for burn victims.

You want an example of God's strange ways? How about flab turning into something that heals and saves lives? Incredible.

Thank you for blessing the overstuffed body of Mr. Genz, Lord. We know that with you all things are possible. Amen.

MARNEE'S HOME (2)

....
Psalm 62:1-8

"Jesus," Marnee prayed, and then she didn't know what to ask. "Jesus," she said again, her hands shaking even though her fingers were twisted together. "Jesus, be with Mom and Dad." She didn't know why she had started with them, why those were her first words. "Thank you that they told me about you because," and then she knew, "because now I can pray. And I think that if I die—" it came to her at the moment that she said it—"I think if I die, I'll be all right. I'll be with you."

She swallowed hard, as if something large had been stuck in her throat. She'd never talked to God like that before—never.

"And help Sarah and Jason. They'll cry. But tell 'em I'm all right with you."

A hundred old pictures danced before her like line drawings coming alive as she thumbed through the pages of her memory: the time she had called Sarah a pig, and the time Jason had cried when she'd taken his bike and not told him. How mad he'd been, the fire in his eyes. It was all there in her mind.

But in spite of some of the arguments they'd had, the three of them were close. Sarah would cry. Jason would tough it out, but inside he'd be screaming too. "I'm sorry," Marnee said, "about dying."

Everything she thought and said in those seconds turned into prayer because Christ was so close beside her that he overheard every last word. For the first time in Marnee's life, Jesus was in her heart, *really* there. He was more than a picture, more than words or ideas. He was real. And he heard every word she said.

Marnee could feel the plane continue to fall emptily, racing toward the crash she'd already seen in her mind—a ball of flame rising like a cloud. She looked around. She'd forgotten the people around her. It didn't seem right that so many people—two hundred maybe—had to die just because of a bad engine. God wouldn't allow that, would he?

"I knew it," the rich guy with sideburns said, twisting almost out of his seat. "We're going to die. It's incredible. I knew it."

He wasn't talking to anyone, really. No one was, it seemed, even though loud voices filled the cabin with noise.

Marnee breathed deeply, her hands folded. Death was coming.

"I knew it. This is it already," the man said. "I knew it." He talked to the window.

The plane continued to fall, the voices around her mixed into jabbering. But it was taking so long. She wished it would come more quickly.

"I fly a lot of miles," the man with sideburns said. "I fly a hundred thousand miles a year, and I'm sure this is it."

The man in suspenders took Marnee's hand suddenly, and she held him because she knew he needed her. She knew so much suddenly. It seemed as if she'd grown old in an instant. Everything was so much different. She squeezed his fingers.

Thank you for keeping a hand in our lives, Lord. It's so comforting to know that this world belongs to you—even in the bad times. Thank you for your grace through Christ. Amen.

RANDY

....

Romans 8:28-39

Randy may or may not have been playing chicken that night.

It was homecoming week in our town, and the whole freshman class was out at a shed, making a float for the homecoming parade by stuffing crepe paper into a chicken-wire sculpture mounted on a hayrack.

A couple of guys were hanging out along the tracks when the train came through. Maybe no one really knows exactly what happened that night; but most people, even today, think Randy and his buddies played chicken, daring one another to be the last person to jump across the tracks.

Whatever happened, Randy didn't make it. His body bounced off the rampaging engine like a rag doll.

I was five years old when that happened. I don't remember Randy. I know his sisters somewhat, and I recognize his picture when I see it in the high school album that was dedicated to him. I never knew him, and he never knew me. Yet, his death—what seems like a useless death—taught me something about life.

One expects to bury grandparents, and already at the time Randy died, I'd had a hold of my mother's hand when we went out to the cemetary to lay my grandfather's body into the ground. I knew something, at least, about death before Randy's.

But his death affected the entire town, and it's stayed with me all these years. I think that's because I knew even then that kids aren't supposed to die. Randy, whether or not he was playing chicken, wasn't supposed to be killed by a train during homecoming week. But he was, and death became real to me that week.

God works in mysterious ways, Cowper says in this hymn.

Randy's death must have seemed meaningless to most people.

What reason, people might have asked, would God have for allowing this tragedy?

Was his death meaningless? For me, no. It's a nick against the wall where I mark my growth, a church school lesson I've never forgotten. What's more, if you're reading these very words and if you understand what I'm trying to tell you about Randy and life and death, then Randy's death thirty-five years ago—whether or not it was in a game of chicken—still has meaning, still teaches.

"The bud," Cowper says, "may have a bitter taste, but sweet will be the flower." Randy's death, even today, is not made sweet by its having taught me something important; but today, all these years later, I know what Cowper means.

God's ways are sometimes mysterious all right. But the words on this page are proof that even the most sad and memorable deaths may not be as meaningless as they seem.

Dear Lord, sometimes it takes us years and years to understand why bad things happen to good people. Sometimes we never figure out your purpose. Comfort all of those who are torn up by tragedy today, wherever they may be. Bring them your Spirit to guide and hold them. Amen.

NOW THANK WE ALL OUR GOD

1 Now thank we all our God with heart and hands and voic - es,
2 O may this boun-teous God through all our life be near us,
3 All praise and thanks to God the Fa - ther now be giv - en,

who won-drous things has done, in whom his world re - joic - es;
with ev - er joy - ful hearts and bless - ed peace to cheer us,
the Son and Spir - it blest, who reign in high - est heav - en—

who from our moth-ers' arms has blessed us on our way
to keep us in his grace, and guide us when per - plexed,
the one e - ter - nal God, whom heaven and earth a - dore;

with count-less gifts of love, and still is ours to - day.
and free us from all ills of this world in the next.
for thus it was, is now, and shall be ev - er - more.

Text: Martin Rinkart, 1636; tr. Catherine Winkworth, 1863, alt.
Tune: Johann Crüger, 1647; harm. based on Felix Mendelssohn's Lobgesang, Opus 52, 1840

67 67 66 66
NUN DANKET

MARNEE'S HOME (3)

....
Psalm 23

Marnee didn't try to pull her hand away when the guy in suspenders grabbed it. She knew he needed her.

"You've got to be terrified," he told her. "You've got to be scared out of your mind." His glasses exaggerated his eyes' pale gray, but he had a smart face, a handsome face with a heavy mustache that spread over his lip when he chewed it. "You're so young," he told her. "You must be scared."

As if it were teasing them, the plane righted itself again, even though it kept falling and falling. . .

"I'll be all right," she said, but he didn't seem to hear.

"I've got this cat," he told her. "She's shut up at home—in the closet with this big tank of water and a cake pan full of food. Nobody's going to think of that cat," he said. "I'll be dead as a nail, and nobody'll think of the puss."

He turned her hand over in his so that his palm faced up. Marnee wanted to tell him what she felt—that she was in God's hand, but all around them people's voices seemed hurried, burdened with huge and heavy fear.

"I'm going to crash, and I end up worried about my cat," he said. "Is that dumb or what?"

The pilot's voice came solidly through the cabin, warning them that they were about to land. Then the plane fell sideways again, slashing through the clouds until Marnee saw fields and trees broken by a river rising at them, thickening as they fell. Life was flying by.

"I never made it to where I wanted to be," the guy said. "I never had the chance. One more year and I'd be in vet school. One lousy year. Can you believe it? I'm going down one year short."

"We're going to be all right," Marnee said. "I know it. We're going to be just fine." She *didn't* know, but she felt she had to reassure the man who held her hand.

NOW THANK WE ALL OUR GOD

They leaned forward to put their heads down, and it surprised her when she felt the wetness on his face. Prayers like chants shimmered through the silence in the cabin as all of them waited to crash. But once again the plane leveled itself, and when Marnee stole a glance out the window, she saw swirling red lights all over the field beneath them.

"It'll be all right," she said, leaning toward him, but his head was down in his left hand. "Do you believe in God?" she asked. "Pray with me," she told him. "Just pray."

He was crying. "Okay," he said.

"Ask God for help," she told him. "Just talk to him."

His hands up at his face seemed to keep him from speaking. She wished so much he'd know what she felt, the comfort.

"Pray?" he said. "I'm going to die."

Father, we know that even when we walk through the valley of the shadow of death, you are with us. Thank you for being our Shepherd. Amen.

THANKS—REALLY!

······································

Habakkuk 3:17-19

Although most of you probably never heard of the Thirty Years War, you can rest assured it was, like most wars, terribly messy. No Rambo stuff. This excerpt from Cicely Wedgewood's history of that war may be all you wish to read:

> At Calw the pastor saw a woman gnawing the raw flesh off a dead horse on which a hungry dog and some ravens were also feeding. . . . In Rhineland [city magistrates] watched the graveyards against marauders who sold the flesh of the newly buried for food . . . . Acorns, goats' skins, grass, were all cooked in Alsace; cats, dogs, and rats were sold in the market at Worms. . . .

People suffered all right. Political and religious hatred teamed up in a particularly rowdy fashion to create a war in which the Austrians and Swedes and just about anyone else looking for power on the continent took turns thrashing the very life out of the German people and countryside.

To those who lived through it, the steel wheels of that war must have seemed to grind on endlessly. Thousands deserted farms and homes for protection in the old walled-in cities. But, soon enough, there was no room. At Strassburg, Ms. Wedgwood says, the living shut their windows to death groans just outside. In winter, people stepped over dead bodies left lying all over the streets. Finally, when the city knew it could do no more, the magistrates threw out 35,000 refugees to the terror and death that would stalk them outside the walls.

Spring came in long days of warm rains that kept the earth moist and rich for disease that flourished in the hot summer sun that followed. Plagues wound through the streets in gusts of warm wind. Outside the gates, law and order crumbled into chaos as men formed marauding, outlaw gangs that killed for food.

Sometime toward the end of this Thirty Years War, picture a man named Martin Rinkert, a servant of God, a preacher in his own hometown, Eilenberg, Saxony. In 1637, at the height of the destruction, thick in the swamp of life-draining disease, Rinkert, the only clergyman left in the city, held funerals for up to fifty people per day. Even his wife died of disease.

But sometime during those years—during the groaning persistence of war's evil—Martin Rinkert sat and wrote this magnificent, stately tribute of thanksgiving to his God, the ruler of a world that appeared to be crumbling.

Thanksgiving! In the middle of all that.

"Now thank we all our God," he wrote, his nostrils full of the stench of death. In spite of all the horror that surrounded him, the man was *still* counting his blessings.

Now that's a testimony! That's faith.

....

Dear Father, thank you for your countless gifts of love. Give us the faith to see your love and faithfulness even on our darkest days—as Martin Rinkert did. Help us to thank you always with heart and hand and voice. Amen.

SUPERSWINE AND OTHER SILLINESS

....

Psalm 19:1-6

We've had Superman, of course, and Mighty Mouse, but I think the cartoon world is now ready for Superpig. Of course, I *would*, living in Iowa.

The notion of Superpig may not sound particularly romantic to some of you, but out here on the prairie, lots of very nice people raise very nice families on malodorous feedlots full of pigs. Out here a new cartoon featuring a hog built like a middle linebacker would get tons of viewers.

Actually, some scientists *are* trying to develop Superpig, but they aren't thinking about cartoons. What's on their minds is the production of pork. They begin by isolating the gene responsible for growth in hogs. Then they glue that extra gene onto the genetic table of baby test-tube pigs and wait for Superhog to emerge.

Now the dream of hogs ten times bigger than normal is quite appealing, especially in flatland like the Midwest. Just think what kind of tourist industry Superpig might create. Some city kid is traveling along with his family. He looks out the window, turns green, and says, "Look, Ma, there's a hippo in that duck pond."

Superhogs could turn the midwestern prairies into the African veld. Iowa becomes Zimbabwe.

I'm pulling your leg.

The reason for Superpig is actually quite simple. Right now it takes about five and a half months—from the day the little curly-tails are born—to get them pumped full of iron and ready for their fateful day at the market. Inside of those months, ordinary pigs eat as much as eight hundred pounds of expensive grain. If Superpig were to grow ten times faster than normal hogs, Mr. and Ms. Farmer would turn over some healthy profits.

But so far those genetic engineers haven't been too successful. Sometimes the gene doesn't "take"—that is, the test-tube pig grows up slowly to look like any other fat pink pig. When the gene does seem to affect the animal, the results haven't been good. The extra gene makes the pigs almost goofy with problems. It turns hogs into hypochondriacs. At least for the time being Superpig may make a better cartoon dream than a feedlot reality.

I don't doubt that some research genius someday will figure out a way to make pigs into American bison, but for right now I'm kind of happy that Superpigs aren't strong-arming every feedlot in Iowa. I like the idea that humanity's best efforts at retooling God's creation sometimes turn out to be hairbrained silliness. God is still the greatest architect. He set the delicate balance of a pig's genetic formation. He gave cats the deadly silence of retractable claws. He gave the slow-footed skunk an offensive weapon. He engineered an incredible combination of three odd-shaped bones at the sides of our heads that allow us to hear.

God nudged the most beautiful and gentle rolls into prairie flatland. He carved out deep valleys and soaring mountains.

Like the song says, his world—even the smelly old feedlot swine—rejoices in him. Even the hogs bring him praise!

....

Everything has your stamp on it, Lord, even our hogs. Give us the kind of vision that sees your glory in the little things, and even the ugly things, of life. Amen.

GRANDMA'S LAST THANKSGIVING

....

Psalm 92:1-4

Once upon a time women weren't supposed to wear slacks to church because some people thought only dresses were proper.

Not my grandma. She liked the wrinkle-free double-knit slacks because they stretched enough through the seat to allow her to sit easily in a folding chair—and they almost always held their press. One winter afternoon my Grandma said not wearing slacks to church was foolish and went off to Ladies Aid in her double-knits.

Grandma never walked too fast, so she must have made quite a spectacle waltzing into that fellowship room. But no one said a thing, and the Bible study likely plodded along as usual, most of the women nodding at most everything the preacher said.

After the preacher closed with prayer, a couple of the women got up to set out the coffee and cookies.

"Why, Mabel," Alma said, "I just can't believe you're wearing pants in church."

Grandma raised an eyebrow. "Oh, this ain't the first time," she said. "I been wearing pants for years."

Always brimming with jokes, Grandma delighted in pulling fast ones. And yet, when I remember Grandma every Thanksgiving, the effect is always serious, never playful.

When she was getting older, she was the holiday's queen. Even now, many years after her death, the smell of a roast turkey reminds me of how she used to stand at the table behind the chairs while everyone was seated, then look around at her family and nod, as if heaven itself were only a block down the sidewalk.

I wasn't home for her last Thanksgiving. My sister's family had her over, along with my parents. But in my imagination I can create the scene—the table drawn out into the living room, the inviting smell of turkey and stuffing wafting through the rooms, the tinkling of forks against my sister's china.

When it was over, Grandma slowly leaned into the car and sat beside my parents on the trip home. She told them it was a good Thanksgiving. Then, her head fell sideways, and my father, sensing something bad, sped to the hospital, where she died.

She played this last little joke on us, dying when she did, so that every Thanksgiving her memory haunts our holiday.

But that's okay. Thanksgiving becomes too easily a recital of "things we have": good health, good food, a nice house, two TVs, a computer, school, friends, church, and a tape deck.

Somehow, Grandma's death on Thanksgiving reminds me of the silliness of such recitals. It reminds me of what God gave her—joy in life through faith not earned but given freely.

Thanksgiving is a fine, harvest custom, but gratitude owns no special date on any calendar. For believers, gratitude is a whole wardrobe, not just a moth-balled costume for October or November use.

I like to think Grandma knows she's still Thanksgiving's queen. And I like to think that up there on the right hand where she's got her place at the table today, she still chuckles about that last fast one she pulled.

And nods—the way she used to right before the meal. Today, heaven, for her, is no longer a block away.

....

Dear Lord, it's easy to thank you for long vacations and new cars. It's not always so easy to thank you for the things in our lives that aren't so thrilling. Help us to work at thanksgiving every day of the year. Amen.

TIME AND ETERNITY

....
Psalm 90:1-6

The Giant Dipper, an almost fifty-year-old roller coaster on the Boardwalk at Santa Cruz, California, has been in the movies. In fact, it's become something of a celebrity. Maybe that's why it takes so long to get through the line to ride the crazy thing.

Time, Einstein says, is relative. After riding the Giant Dipper, I know what he means.

My son and I chugged slowly up and down the long aisles leading to the roller coaster, waiting for what seemed forever before finally setting our feet in the Dipper. But once we were seated, everything seemed to go almost too quickly.

The celebrity roller coaster bolted down into a midnight alley, swerved and jerked and turned in complete darkness. All we could do was hang on. The Dipper charged out into the daylight, inched up an incline and then threw itself over the edge. Suddenly my stomach flattened itself into a soggy pancake somewhere around the level of my throat. Whoever could, moaned. Twisting and dipping like something alive, that coaster rolled over humps and dipped through bellies wildly . . . until it finally slowed us down and came to a halt.

We'd stood in line for a half hour (at least!), waiting for a ride that took no longer (I thought) than thirty seconds. Some kid next to us said the Giant Dipper ride was actually two whole minutes long. I couldn't believe it. Maybe that's what people mean when they say "Time flies when you're having fun."

Time, people say, is relative. They're wrong, of course.

Seconds ticked off during that wild ride just as quickly as they did when we stood "forever" in line. Time stops for no man, woman, or Giant Dipper.

In April of 1513, Ponce de Leòn first set his Spanish feet on Florida soil while looking for something called the Fountain of Youth. He never found the fountain, of course, but thousands of senior citizens, trying to slow time down, think it's still down there somewhere between the coasts.

Sometimes it seems that people will do almost anything to halt the outward evidence of passing time. Men and women flock to plastic surgeons for face lifts that will erase the telltale lines that creep around the eyes and mouth. Older men wear gold chains that they hope will make them look like Tom Selleck. Older women try new fashion trends and new hair colors that they hope will make them look younger. Time may seem relative, but everyone really knows better.

In an old Greek myth, Aurora, goddess of the dawn, falls head over heels for Tithonus, a good-looking guy who is, unfortunately, mortal. Aurora pleads with Jupiter to allow her sweetheart to escape death, and Jupiter agrees. But Aurora forgets to ask for the one thing that will make Tithonus's eternal life bearable: eternal youth.

The years pass and Tithonus gets old, loses his hair—and Aurora, his young love. Gradually he also loses his strength and eventually the use of his arms and legs. The horror of the story is that time keeps whaling away on him, and he can't escape. He can't die.

Somebody ought to make that myth into a movie.

The last word of this hymn is one that we have no way of understanding clearly because we're all creatures of time.

Eternity—what it's like—is something known only to God. Only Christ is really able to make time relative for us.

Father, we know that you have no beginning and no end, that for you a thousand years are like a day. Thank you for sending your Son to redeem us from the limited time of this world and to bring us to live eternally with you. In his name, Amen.

MARNEE'S HOME (4)

....
Psalm 107:1-9

Her hand in the tight clasp of the man beside her, Marnee peeked out and saw the lights on the runway slowly rise to meet them. Her eyes clenched, she pushed her head down to her knees, waiting. "Lord," she said, "let him live. Take me if you want to, but let this guy live. He doesn't know."

The whole line of seats bucked from the floor as the plane skipped up off the surface like a flat rock off water, then slapped down again, tires shrieking. But it did settle down; the plane straightened itself as if it were being toed. Marnee sat up quickly and looked out.

Fire retardant, like slush on the cement, splashed up around the tires. They'd made it. They were down. They weren't going to crash.

"We're down," she said. "You hear me?—We're down."

The guy beside her raised his head and looked around, squinting. "I'm not flying again," he said. "Never."

Marnee leaned back as the plane slowed its charge down the runway. She squeezed the man's hand, then pulled away and brought both her hands up to her face, covering her eyes.

She thanked God in the blurting kind of prayer she'd made since the moment the plane first fell, the words pouring out.

"God Almighty, thank you—thank you so much," she said. And when there were no more words, she kept her eyes tightly shut so that her silence could carry her gratitude.

When the plane came to a stop, the flight attendant rushed the passengers down the emergency chutes, and they ran—all of them— toward the nearest hanger. Marnee lost her friend in the dash to get away. Fearing an explosion, she ran for her life in the swell of the mob.

Later, in the airport, bright TV cameras turned the gate into a circus. All of the reporters wanted interviews. "What was it like to think you were going to die?" they asked her, but Marnee turned her head and moved on through the gate.

Once they were safe, once they stood with their feet beneath them on the bright red airport rug, the passengers wept openly. Marnee felt the burning on her cheeks and made no attempt to stop her tears. It felt wonderful to cry—like long breaths on the ground after sprints.

She could call her parents and tell them now, finally, that she was coming home. It seemed so different to call the new place home. But it was. Now she knew it.

She was going to live—a second chance. It would be different now, she told herself as she looked for a phone.

Father, we know that you hear all of our cries and whispers. We know that you have the power to push storms aside and cradle airplanes in your hand. We praise you for the miracles that bring us closer to you and thank you for your abundant mercy and grace.
In Jesus' name, Amen.

GUIDE ME, O MY GREAT REDEEMER

1 Guide me, O my great Re - deem - er, pil - grim through this
2 O - pen now the crys - tal foun - tain, where the heal - ing
3 When I tread the verge of Jor - dan, bid my anx - ious

bar - ren land; I am weak, but you are might - y;
wa - ters flow. Let the fire and cloud - y pil - lar
fears sub - side. Death of death, and hell's De - struc - tion,

hold me with your power - ful hand. Bread of heav - en, bread of heav - en,
lead me all my jour - ney through. Strong De - liv - erer, strong De - liv - erer,
land me safe on Ca - naan's side. Songs of prais - es, songs of prais - es

feed me now and ev - er - more, feed me now and ev - er - more.
ev - er be my strength and shield, ev - er be my strength and shield.
I will ev - er sing to you, I will ev - er sing to you.

Text: William Williams, 1745; st. 1 tr. Peter Williams, 1771, alt.; st. 2–3 tr. William Williams, 1772, alt.
Tune: John Hughes, 1907

87 87 877
CWM RHONDDA

HARMONY

....
Ephesians 4:4-13

Turning a double play is an art.

A runner's on first when a ground ball is hit to second. The shortstop has to make several split-second decisions—how to get to the bag at the exact moment the throw does, which side of the bag to hit, and how to get his own throw over or around the runner.

But that's not all. For the play to work smoothly, the second basemen has to know what decisions the shortstop is making. The two need to work in harmony. That's the art of the double play: two players thinking—playing—as if they were one.

Dancers need to work in harmony too. Forty years ago Fred Astaire and Ginger Rogers danced their way through a shelf full of movies. Together, across a stage or though a moonlit garden, their bodies moved in perfect harmony.

Our word *harmony* comes from the old Greek word *harmos*, meaning "a joining or a fitting." Whether you see it or hear it in singing or dancing or making double plays, harmony happens when two or more things fit together, agree.

A woman I know who grew up In a church where the people sang psalms without an organ claims that sometimes today she misses the old way of singing because, she says, in her old church people learned to harmonize, to fit together.

There is something great about harmony, something haunting. You can feel it when you sing a round in church, each side's notes turning and spinning through each other to make the sound deeper and richer, transforming it into something almost alive.

My mother's family used to sit around our living room and sing together—sometimes happy little verses and sometimes silly songs. But the songs you couldn't laugh about are the ones I remember best— songs such as my grandpa's favorite, "Beautiful Savior." My uncles and aunts would sing those special songs in harmony, and after the last note drifted from the room, no one would speak for a while. They would sit there for a second in silence—as if there were no words to describe the beauty.

The Welsh have the grandest tradition of harmony I know.

Sometimes ten thousand Welsh people get together to make music, to harmonize, in a gathering they call a *Cymanfu Ganu*. Even in North America great armies of Welsh still gather to sing.

"Guide Me, O My Great Redeemer" is a hymn written by a Welshman for a *Cymanfu Ganu*. Its melody, a tune called CWM RHONDDA, is named after the the Rhondda river valley in the coal-mining district of Wales—a place where a great singing festival took place in the early part of this century.

Next time you sing this hymn, think of the song that way—as if a thousand people were joining voices the way people join hands, fitting together in harmony.

In two thousand years of Christendom God's people have created lots of dreams of heaven—streets paved with gold, fat little angels winging around with harps and flutes, all kinds of folks in white robes singing, hours on end. Maybe there will be more than that. Maybe there will be dancing. Maybe some ballplayers will be turning double plays.

But my guess is, one way or another, we'll harmonize. We'll fit together like we've never fit before.

Lord, our congregations and denominations often lack harmony. We place more energy into getting our own way than into trying to conform our way to yours. Help us to work together in harmony, looking forward to the day when we'll all fit together perfectly in your eternal kingdom. Amen.

DIRECTIONS FOR PILGRIMS

....
Hebrews 11:8-10

When we sing "Guide Me, O My Great Redeemer," we confess that we are pilgrims.

This old Welsh hymn is something like another old song I remember, one that goes like this:

> I am a stranger here
> within a foreign land;
> my home is far away
> upon a golden strand.

I remember singing those words when I was a little boy.

You may not agree with me, but today those lyrics make me pull up my nose. In fact, I wouldn't sing that song anymore. It's not that I don't like calling myself a stranger, or a pilgrim—anyone who takes faith in God seriously is going to feel at odds with the world around him sometimes. Some nights I wonder, for instance, if what I watch on television or in the movies is "good" for me—you know what I mean? Not that I don't like what I see. Sometimes I do. But maybe that's part of the problem.

So I don't mind thinking of myself as a pilgrim, someone my dictionary defines as one who "journeys in alien lands," because most of the time I know I'm not like most TV characters. What makes me pull up my nose about that old song is the way those lyrics suggest that this world we're in isn't worth a nickel.

This world is, after all, God's. He owns it because he made it. It's got its ugliness all right—I don't have to wallow in the muck to illustrate—but it's got its promise, too. It's God's world. And because he put us in it, he wants us here, working, being his people.

That's why I no longer feel comfortable singing a song that suggests we just throw in the towel on this world and point our snoots toward heaven. That's not only silly—it's sinful.

In today's Scripture passage the pilgrim Abraham is remembered for turning his back on the world and following God's direction into a new and alien land. But did Abraham turn his back on living? Of course not. He lived in tents, had kids, raised thousands of sheep and cattle, and became so great that even the Hittites (Gen. 23:6) called him a "mighty prince among us." That doesn't sound like a man who quit living to sit around longing for heaven. Abraham, I'm sure, longed for heaven, but he didn't turn his back on life. On sin, yes. On life—and the world God gave him, no.

My family and I just returned from a trip to California. If you've ever crossed the southwest deserts, you know what the song means when it calls land "barren." I remember one spot where a sign claimed that the next gas station was a hundred-and-fifty miles away. Sometimes we'd ride for two or three blazing hours without seeing a house or a barn. That land is barren.

The evening news is often barren too: A man is convicted of manslaughter in the death of his fifteen-month-old daughter; the drought continues; AIDS worries medical authorites as it grows among the populace; a football star admits to drug abuse.

Sometimes this tough world looks bleak and barren, a place Christians wouldn't want to live. But pilgrims are workers.

They don't throw in the towel. "Guide Me, O My Great Redeemer," the song says, because, like Abraham, we're going to work, not quit. We're going to follow God's direction in building his kingdom.

....
O equip us for life, dear Lord. You give us life, and
you present us with this world in all of its ugliness
and glory. Help us to live for you in every last thing
we do. Lead us to reflect your light in a barren land.
Amen.

GUIDANCE

....
Psalm 48

Okay, vocabulary quiz. Which of the following is the best definition of a *sextant?*

a. a mutation of the six-legged species of bog fly called *mungus phobus;*

b. an instrument used for measuring angles in stars;

c. a church custodian charged with keeping the grounds and sanctuary prepared for meetings;

d. a criminal convicted of extremely naughty things.

No matter how appealing the rest of these definitions are, the answer, as the wizards among you already know, is b. For centuries, the sextant was an essential tool for any bearded sea captain ready to ship out on the high seas. The sextant measures the angles between the stars and the horizon and thus helps pinpoint exactly where a ship is.

A *compass* is another tool that travelers use to find their way. If you've backpacked out in the High Sierras or the Rocky Mountains, you've likely used this small device with a tippy magnetized needle that always points north. Compass in hand, one at least knows north from south.

High tech has put both the compass and the sextant in museums—not because these old instruments don't work, but because today we have faster and more accurate ways of finding out where we are.

The people of Israel had no high tech—and no sextants or compasses either. When Pharoah gave them the green light to leave Egypt and Moses tiptoed them across the Jordan, they had no way of determining which direction was which. They became pilgrims, wanderers, followers of a promise that Moses relayed to them from God—that somewhere out there lay a promised land, a home.

But, as our hymn says, God gave his people guidance, a pillar of cloud and a pillar of fire (Ex. 13:21). And when they were hungry, he laid the ground white with manna.

I don't know a soul today who is out in the wilderness trying to figure out his or her position. There may be open space at the North and South Poles, but for the most part the world's wildernesses are pretty well mapped.

I know, however, that there are still a lot of folks who need guidance—even Christians.

That's what makes this hymn the prayer of so many—we all want guidance, a sure sense of footing down the paths that lie before us, the kind of guidance that God gave the people of Israel. We want to know which school to go to, which friends to hang around with, what courses to choose, which job to take, what to do with the rest of our lives, who to date, how to deal with parents (or children!).

But today God doesn't work in fiery pillars. So sometimes it's difficult to figure out which way he's guiding us. Sometimes God's will for our lives is mysterious. If it weren't, this hymn wouldn't be a favorite. If we could just call up God's will on a computer screen, we wouldn't be asking him to guide us.

But the great thing is, even when we're unsure, we know that God listens to us. We can always call on God, and there's no long-distance charge. He listens. He delivers.

This song is not the cry of the lost—it's a pilgrim's prayer.

Lord, we need your guidance. We often have tough choices to make, and we're unclear about your will for our lives. Please lead us safely through our journey. Amen.

NAMES

....

Romans 6: 5-11

Picture yourself in a real *Cymanfu Ganu*, singing this Welsh, made-for-a-multitude hymn with a couple thousand other people, the organist leaning back, letting out all the stops.

When you get to the last verse, the church shakes. "When I tread the verge of Jordan,/bid my anxious fears subside./Death of death, and hell's Destruction,/land me safe on Canaan's side." Whoops! You're lost. Something doesn't make sense here. You can figure out that the verse says something about approaching death and side-stepping anxious fears. But what on earth does "Death of death and hell's Destruction" mean?

Yesterday we had a vocabulary quiz, today a grammar lesson. Hang in there. Right after this comes recess.

Lesson #1: The whole hymn is a series of commands, eight separate ones, in fact. See if you can find them.

Lesson #2: You've likely already noted that the commands begin with verbs. Commands spoken in English usually do. For instance, "Get your aardvark out of my sink" starts with the verb *get*. In this hymn the commands begin with the verbs *guide*, *hold*, *feed*, *open*, *let*, *be*, *bid*, and *land*.

Lesson #3: A sentence that contains a command often has no subject; the subject is understood: "(Benny) get up!"

However, commands sometimes contain words or phrases that modify the subject: "Get out of bed, you two-toed sloth."

Lesson #4: Such phrases as "two-toed sloth," called appositives, rename the command's subject. This hymn has five such appositives. "O my great Redeemer" is one. "Bread of heaven" (st. 1) is another; it refers to Christ, who, like manna to the Israelites, has become our own bread (John 6:31-35).

"Strong Deliverer" (st. 2), the third appositive, needs no explanation.

The fourth and fifth appositives are the phrases that puzzled us in stanza 3: "Death of death and hell's Destruction."

These strange phrases also "rename" the subject of the commands. Christ is, in fact, the "Death of death." When he rose from the grave, he walked all over death, ended it, killed it.

He is also "hell's Destruction"—he destroyed hell for all who have faith in him. One of the really frightening things about hell is that it lasts a long, long time. In fact, forever. It can't be toppled. Yet, Christ destroyed hell for believers. For us, hell is no more to fear, say, than Oskaloosa.

For hundreds of years Christians have tried to describe this sometimes mysterious God, and in the process they have created long lists of names and appositives. You might think of Isaiah's roster, for instance: "Wonderful, Counselor, the Mighty God, the Everlasting Father, the Prince of Peace."

William Williams, the author of this hymn, may have had a rather undistinguished name himself, but he did add a few new titles to the ever-growing list given to God the Father: "Death of death" and "hell's Destruction."

They are titles that put peace in the hearts of believers.

....

*Dear Lord, nothing is as scary as death. But we
know that because of your great victory on the cross
we no longer have to fear death or hell. You are truly
the "Death of death" and "hell's Destruction."
Amen.*

MARNEE'S HOME (5)

....

Psalm 116: 1-7

She didn't even know where they'd landed—just some place on the way to Arizona. Inside the restroom, she stared at herself in the mirror and watched tears rim around the corners of her eyes. Somehow it felt so good to cry.

She stood in line for what seemed like hours at the telephone, waiting, gazing up at the clock. Omaha, Nebraska, the signs said. She could tell her parents they were in Omaha. As the line dwindled, Marnee could hear what others were saying on the phone. One man swore at the airlines, and another cried happily. The grandma right in front of her smiled the whole time she told the horrible story, trying to reassure her grandchildren who clung to her hands.

Finally it was Marnee's turn. The phone rang twice, three times—then six, seven. It occured to her that her parents might already have left for the airport, but she let the phone ring anyway, time after time after time, even though a dozen people still stood in line behind her. The whole crash story sat on the very tip of her tongue. There was so much to say—how she'd prayed and how she'd talked to the man beside her, and how it was finally over. How she'd seen death.

"Listen," the guy behind her said. "Why don't you let it go for a minute. Let me talk and then try it again."

She had to let it stop ringing. "Maybe they're not home," she said, as if to excuse herself. "I don't know."

"Hang around," he said. "Just hang around."

She stepped away and watched the lines still stacked behind the phones. If she had only heard her mother's voice, that alone would have been enough. But fear still crept into her, made her shaky.

She saw the guy in suspenders leaning up against the wall and holding a drink. When he saw her, he came over and smiled, pointing his glass when he spoke. "Hey, little girl," he said. "We made it—you and me. I thought we were carbon!" Marnee wiped at her eyes as if there were still tears.

"You almost had me praying—you realize that?" he said, mouthing the swizzle stick from his drink. "If I wasn't so scared, I would'a been. I can't believe it yet. It's amazing what a little fear can do." Then he broke into a laugh.

"Listen," he said, "don't take that stuff seriously, hear? What we just went through was like a bad dream, nothing to get all spacey about. People do screwy things. You know what I mean?" He tipped his glass toward her.

"I'm sorry," she said, even though she didn't know why.

"That's all right," he told her. "Like I say, times like that nobody's really responsible for what they do." He looked around, up and down the rows of people. "You want a drink?"

She shook her head. "I'm too young," she said.

Maybe he was right, she thought miserably. After all, almost dying hadn't seemed to affect him. Maybe the whole thing was only a bad dream. Maybe her prayers had been meaningless.

Hundreds of people milled all around her, but she'd never felt so alone as she did that moment, huddled against the wall, holding her purse.

....

Dear Father, reassure us of your presence. Remind us that you hear our cries and guide us through all of life's trials and dangers. Keep us safe in your hand, free from the doubt and fear that fill our world. In your powerful name, Amen.

THEME
55

LEAD ON, O KING ETERNAL

1 Lead on, O King e - ter - nal, the day of march has come;
2 Lead on, O King e - ter - nal, till sin's fierce war shall cease,
3 Lead on, O King e - ter - nal; we fol - low, not with fears,

hence - forth in fields of con - quest your tents will be our home.
and ho - li - ness shall whis - per the sweet a - men of peace.
for glad - ness breaks like morn - ing wher - e'er your face ap - pears.

Through days of prep - a - ra - tion your grace has made us strong;
For not with swords' loud clash - ing or roll of stir - ring drums—
Your cross is lift - ed o'er us, we jour - ney in its light;

and now, O King e - ter - nal, we lift our bat - tle song.
with deeds of love and mer - cy the heav - en-ly king-dom comes.
the crown a - waits the con - quest; lead on, O God of might.

Text: Ernest W. Shurtleff, 1888, alt.
Tune: Henry T. Smart, 1836

76 76 D
LANCASHIRE

MARCHING SONGS

....

Ephesians 6:10-17

The church I attended as a boy had a bell up front on the piano—one of those little silver domes you ring by smashing it with your palm. At half past eleven the Sunday school superintendent used to bang that bell to get all the classes assembled and ready to sing.

After picking a number himself, he'd ask for favorites, and every week we'd beg for the same song: "449," one of us would yell. Something about the hymn "Onward, Christian Soldiers" chugged along with our sense of fun.

Back then World War II was fairly recent history. Most of the kids—including me—who sang "Onward Christian Soldiers" every Sunday could go upstairs to the attic and slip into their dad's old army khakis or navy blues.

Now World War II was a horrible war, but it had clear favorites. The guys with the black hats—without any doubt—were the Axis powers: Germany and Japan. The good guys were the rest of the free world. To kids who grew up with a fresh memory of Hitler's horrors, war itself seemed quite righteous. It wasn't hard, when I was a kid, to think that Christians were soldiers. In fact, it sounded very right—fighters, bayoneting sin.

Not so today. In Vietnam, the United States simply did not win. What's more, the long, drawn-out horror of that war turned soldiers into villians instead of heroes. In Vietnam, no one wore white hats. Lots of people—including myself— started wondering if real Christians could fight in that war, could stand out on a field and shoot another human being. Some Christians did everything they could to avoid going to Vietnam.

Today, hardly anyone asks to sing "Onward, Christian Soldiers" anymore—not because the music is bad but because the idea of a "Christian soldier" is harder to imagine than it was when the tracks of

Allied tanks still lay fresh in the European soil. Besides, the Sermon on the Mount says Christians make peace, not war.

So today, most hymns that use the idea of Christian warriors—including the hymn we want to look at this week, "Lead On, O King Eternal"—seem out of fashion. "Day of march," "fields of conquest," "tents," and "battle song"—all these phrases are straight out of war. So if war itself seems unChristian to you, you probably don't like this hymn any more than you like old #449.

But "Lead On, O King Eternal" wasn't written some night on a smoky battlefield. It was written by a young American in the late 1800s to be sung on graduation night by his own seminary class. To Ernest W. Shurtleff "days of preparation" referred not to bayonet practice but to those long hot mornings of hitting the Greek and Hebrew books. "Fields of conquest" didn't mean bloody, pock-marked battlefields lined with muddy trenches. To a class of future preachers, "fields of conquest" were the mission fields that awaited them, places thronging with people waiting to hear the clear and hopeful trumpet blast of the gospel of Christ.

So you don't have to be in a war to love "Lead On, O King Eternal"— but you probably have to be a soldier of the cross.

Dear Lord, we live in a world scarred by wars and violence, and we long for peace. Yet we know that the struggle against evil will go on until you come again. Arm us with shields of faith so that we may show others the way to the peace that is ours through your sacrifice. Amen.

ROOTS

....

Ruth 1:8-18

At times, one can tell the Reverend Ernest W. Shurtleff had his classmates specifically in mind when he wrote this hymn. For instance, when he says in the first verse "your tents will be our home," he's alluding to one of the facts of preachers' lives—they usually move, and do it quite often.

In fact, Shurtleff himself never put down roots. Listen to his life's itinerary:

In 1887, he started out in Ventura, California.

Just a few years later he took a new church in Plymouth, Massachusetts, all the way across the continent.

And that wasn't the end. Seven years later he took his family to a church on the icy northern plains of Minneapolis, Minnesota.

In twenty years, he'd served three churches, one on each coast and another right smack in between.

But don't close the book. There's more. In 1905 he went to Frankfurt, Germany, of all places, and started an American church.

And that still wasn't the end. By the time World War I rolled around, Shurtleff had found his way to Paris, where he and his wife worked tirelessly among the casualties of what some people still call "The Great War."

It's possible that Rev. Mr. Shurtleff hated moving. My guess, on the basis of what he said in his graduation hymn, is that moving was something he simply considered to be a part of the territory that came with the job—fringe benefit, so to speak.

"Your tents will be our home" suggests the kind of living quarters whose canvas walls are hardly permanent. In a tent, you put down stakes, but no roots. That makes it possible to move easily and efficiently.

When my wife and I were married, we gathered up every last scrap of important junk we had and stuck it all—plus camping gear and food—into a 4' x 6' U-Haul trailer and moved to the Southwest. I remember the dying heaves of my Volkswagon's engine as we lugged that trailer up staggeringly long grades in the Rockies. At times I wanted to get out and walk alongside my vehicle, as if I were an old homesteader trying to make the prairie schooner a little lighter for the sweaty oxen. That trailer was so heavy.

Today, sixteen years later, we couldn't get the stuff we've got in the basement laundry room into a 4' x 6' trailer. Maybe TNT could move all the things we've accumulated through the years, but the sheer bulk of what we own makes moving seem nightmarish.

I wonder sometimes whether "tents will by our home" isn't really meant for all of us, not just for the Rev. Mr. Shurtleff's seminary buddies or ministers in general. Because I sometimes wonder whether God's voice gets muffled between the overstuffed pillows of all our front-room furniture.

Be careful when you sing "your tents will be our home."

Be sure you know what you're saying. Rev. Shurtleff is asking us to pledge a great deal here—nothing less than to follow Christ.

....

Help us not to put too much importance on what we have, Lord, because we really have nothing. We'll take nothing along out of this life, nothing at all. Keep us in tents so that we can be your foot soldiers. In Jesus' name, Amen.

MARNEE'S HOME (6)

....

Jude: 20-24

Marnee paced up and down near the phone booth. Maybe next time she dialed someone would answer, someone would be home. At the desk, her ex-friend in suspenders held his drink like a pro, joking with a stewardess. Even Christ seemed gone now, maybe back on the plane. Marnee felt all alone.

She'd had so many friends just two nights ago on the bus ride home from the tournament game against Hubbard. Her team had lost—which was pretty much what they had expected in a game against Hubbard's fireball pitcher. But even though they hadn't won, everybody on the bus seemed happy—even coach, who was sitting up front with Molly the driver, throwing jokes back every once in a while like a kid.

And singing. The whole team started on a bunch of dopey songs, the kind you sing when you're jumping rope: "Sally and Terry sitting in a tree." That kind. Then Coach started the golden oldies—the Beach Boys. She stood up in the aisle and belted out the first verse of "California Girls." Everybody about died laughing.

Finally, they sang the "Friends" song, and Marnee knew it was meant for her. Sherry sat with her arm around Marnee's shoulders, and, even though the bus was roaring down the freeway, the whole team came up and hugged her.

She'd had so many friends, she thought. Dozens.

And then the last song—a round. Coach started it. She was the kind of person who lived her Christianity instead of just talking about it all the time. She started a round that they had sung hundreds of times in chapel—"Praise and Thanksgiving." Only on that night it had sounded especially beautiful, both sides of the bus bringing their parts together in harmony, making soft, sweet music.

When they had reached the end of the round, Marnee hadn't wanted it to stop so she had stood up and started in again on the first verse. The bus had been full of music.

The third verse came back to Marnee now: "May we go out from here sharing God's love./Help us in coming days our faith to prove." She'd never really thought about what those words meant—until now. Sweet harmony had kept the words inside Marnee's head, but they'd really meant nothing until she was alone in the airport of a town she'd never seen before.

"Help us in coming days our faith to prove." She'd sung it herself, she thought, sung it with tears in her eyes, as if it was really some big commitment. Maybe it was. Of course it was.

And that's when she saw the man who'd sat beside the window on the flight, the man with the sideburns. He was sitting alone in one of those TV chairs, staring at a blank screen.

He looked, to Marnee, frightfully lonely.

Father, thank you for preparing us for each challenge that you send our way. Keep us in your love and help us build ourselves in the faith. In Jesus' name, Amen.

A PICTURE OF CHRIST

························

Psalm 27:1-3

One day in 1940 four German soldiers and their captain marched into a small Christian school in the Netherlands.

The children were afraid. They eyed the soldiers' perfect uniforms, their tall, shiny boots, and their clenched lips.

What the captain said was only partly understandable to the class. He commanded their teacher to obey new rules, new ideas.

He explained that the Germans would be running the schools now that *der Fuhrer* was ruling the Netherlands.

When the Nazis left, the teacher sat behind his desk and tried to collect his breath. His eyes seemed tipped with fear.

The Nazis had already robbed the town of some of its men.

On the way to school one morning, the children had seen a German soldier throw an old man from his bike, then take it and ride away. They knew, already then, that no one could fight the Nazis openly.

"They told me what they wanted here," the teacher said. He held his head in one hand as if he were in pain. "They say, for instance, that that picture must come down." He pointed up at the picture of Christ on the wall opposite the window.

And then his eyes closed, and everyone knew he was praying. Two days later when the Nazis returned, the children knew that their teacher hadn't complied with the new German rules. Up above them on the east wall, the picture of Christ still hung, as if the teacher had forgotten the intruders' commands.

"Take it down," the captain said. One of his men laid his hand on the holster of his pistol. "I ordered it taken down, and I mean it," he said, his hand up in the air toward the ceiling.

Then the children saw something strange fill the teacher's face—a broad and real smile. "I will not," he said. "This is a Christian school. You may do with me what you will. I will not take down that picture."

Twice the Nazi captain threatened, and twice their teacher, his face bright with that smile, shook his head.

Before he left, the Nazi captain walked around among the students, and once or twice ran his fingers through a child's hair. And then he was gone. By some miracle he'd backed down. The picture stayed.

Almost fifty years later one of the boys from that Dutch school walked into a lawyer's office not far from where I'm sitting and told the lawyer that he wanted to will thousands of dollars to the local Christian school, even though his own children had not attended there.

He said he would never forget the way that teacher in that Christian school had stood up for Christ. It stayed with him, he said, for his entire life. And now, so many years later, he wanted some of the blessings God had given him throughout his life to honor the courage of that Christian man.

Thank God for a teacher without a name, a believer who lived outside of fear, his heart with God. "Lead on, O King eternal; we follow, not with fears."

Help us to be fearless, Lord, in our faith. Keep us from feeling that we're just little people, because we aren't. Your love makes us stronger than anything. Thank you for so much, Lord. Amen.

TERROR AND GLORY

....

1 Corinthians 13

When you read these words, what happened yesterday will be almost forgotten—just one of a thousand terrorist acts. Greek officials still aren't sure of the whole story, but it appears that three terrorists somehow boarded a luxury liner and unloaded their machine guns on whoever moved.

Today, nine of the passengers and crew are dead and almost one hundred injured, fifteen still in serious condition. When the gunfire began, panicked passengers jumped ship. Some of those are still being brought in, so an accurate death count isn't yet possible. In the middle of the confusion, the killers slipped away in a speedboat.

To most North Americans today, terrorism has the face of an Arab. Terrorists come in all shapes and sizes and colors, of course, but this afternoon, before anyone had a clear sense of who the murderers could have been, most of the world guessed the cruise-ship machine gunners were Lebanese or Iranian.

There were no soldiers among the victims, of course. Terrorism is murder for effect. Terrorists kill purely innocent people, caught completely unprepared.

Most North Americans, I assume, would have trouble killing a deer in a woods. How is it, then, that some human beings can so effectively erase their own human feelings and kill children indiscriminately, spray entire crowds with bullets, as if what they were throwing around were little more than political phrases?

One answer is a grievance, of course. Loving fathers and mothers don't turn into killers without being angry. Lebanon hates the Israeli occupation; Iran still hates the U.S.

But also, to certain Islamic fundamentalists, terrorism brings its own rewards. Blowing oneself up with a car bomb and destroying fifty or sixty other people in the process is a red-carpet path to glory for a Muslim. Dying in a righteous cause is a way of earning life eternal.

Doesn't this hymn promise the same thing? The final words of the song make the claim "the crown awaits the conquest." It seems to me that line suggests that our warfare earns us a crown of glory. Isn't that the same idea that pushes terrorists?

Perhaps, but only if we avoid singing the second stanza, which explains very clearly that a Christian's great battle is fought with love and mercy, not Uzzis or Stinger missles.

Christian soldiers battle with open hearts rather than bazookas.

Their mission is not to bring death, but, at all costs, life.

And there's another reason, of course. "The crown awaits the conquest" may sound like Islamic promises, but it isn't, and I hope, after all these readings, you know why.

Maybe a Koran-reading fundamentalist is confident of earning his salvation by blowing himself into pieces. But those who believe in Christ know they never will *earn* salvation.

Truly amazing grace is not that which we earn by dying for a righteous cause. What makes amazing grace amazing, remember, is that it comes, perfectly wrapped, as the greatest of gifts. The crown of life awaits us—not because we've earned it, but because it's promised. It's ours, from Christ, free.

No matter how perfect we are, Lord, we don't earn
what you've already given us—freedom from death
and sin through the death of your Son. May our lives
sing with your praise. Amen.

JESUS SHALL REIGN WHERE'ER THE SUN

1 Je - sus shall reign wher - e'er the sun does its suc -
2 To him shall end - less prayer be made, and prais - es
3 Peo - ple and realms of ev - ery tongue dwell on his
4 Bless - ings a - bound wher - e'er he reigns: the pris - oners
5 Let ev - ery crea - ture rise and bring the high - est

ces - sive jour - neys run, his king-dom stretch from
throng to crown his head. His name like sweet per -
love with sweet - est song, and in - fant voic - es
leap to lose their chains, the wea - ry find e -
hon - ors to our King, an - gels de - scend with

shore to shore, till moons shall wax and wane no more.
fume shall rise with ev - ery morn - ing sac - ri - fice.
shall pro - claim their ear - ly bless - ings on his name.
ter - nal rest, and all who suf - fer want are blest.
songs a - gain, and earth re - peat the loud a - men.

Text: Isaac Watts, 1719, alt.; based on Psalm 72
Tune: John Hatton, 1793

LM
DUKE STREET

OUR MISSION

....
Mark 16:14-20

I remember a picture from a book I read thirty years ago, a book called *Through Gates of Splendor.*

I'll never forget the book because of the story behind it, a big news story that ran front page for weeks in every newspaper in the country. Christian missionaries were murdered—martyred, you might say—and one of them was the husband of the author of that book. The missionaries had been bringing the gospel to a jungle tribe named the Aucas, somewhere in Ecuador. For one reason or another, the Aucas turned on them and killed them.

The picture I've never forgotten was a close-up of a grisly looking Auca spear decorated up near the blade with the gospel tracts those missionaries had handed out. The gospel and death. "Jesus Shall Reign" is, above all else, a missionary's hymn, a hymn that I'm sure those men who died in Ecuador knew well. Even today this old hymn marches along like a rallying cry. It's not hard to get cranked up for missions, singing this one.

And that's just what Isaac Watts intended. He wrote this hymn with missions in mind. Originally he also included another stanza—a stanza we don't sing anymore because what it says is in very poor taste. Here's the stanza:

> From north and south the princes meet
> to pay their homage at His feet,
> while Western empires own their Lord
> and savage tribes attend His word.

Maybe you can tell why no one sings that stanza anymore. No? Okay, try to name a "Western empire" (Europe, North America, Australia) that "owns their Lord." (*Own* here means "acknowledge," as in "own up to what you did.") Would a country that officially acknowledges Jesus Christ as its Lord pass a law outlawing prayer in its own schools? Of course not. No "Western" nation calls itself Christian today.

What's more, the final line is more than a little racist.

The word "savage," when it follows the chest-thumping pride of the line before it, turns whoever isn't "Western" and probably white into a blood-thirsty jungle barbarian who slurps up sumptuous meals of enemy stew. We good—you bad.

Three hundred years ago Isaac Watts wrote the song without blushing, because when he saw missions, he saw lily-white people tramping around in the mud to bring the gospel to naked black folks with sticks in their noses or rings in their ears, to savages armed with darts and toting fistfulls of shrunken human heads.

I'll never forget that picture. Missions look exciting when we see spears lined with gospel tracts. To most of us, carrying the word to an African jungle seems more adventuresome than spreading the good news on a Japanese commuter train or in a Denver financial office. But the goal hasn't changed. The jungle is shrinking, but the Great Commission still holds, and Isaac Watts' old hymn still rings—as long as we cut out some poor taste.

We're all missionaries, whether we're slashing through a New Guinea rain forest or fixing our neighbor's toilet. Maybe, just maybe, the greatest mission field is one just outside your back door. You know what they say—it's a jungle out there.

Lord, please help us to be your witnesses wherever we live or work or play. The mission field that you've given us lies right outside our own living rooms. Give us the love for others that you've shown us in the gift of love you've given us. In the name of your Son who lives, Amen.

MARNEE'S HOME (7)

....
Romans 12:9-15

The man with the sideburns had very little hair. He wore a gray suit with a dark lavender tie and held a thin briefcase at his side, as if he were afraid to let it stand beside the chair.

He stared as if his mind were far away.

"Hi," Marnee said, but he didn't move his eyes. She slid into the chair beside him. "How's it going?" she asked. "Remember me? I sat beside you on the plane? Really bad, wasn't it?"

He looked at her as if he questioned whether she was real.

"I was right beside you," she said. "There was you by the window, and then me in the middle, and the guy in suspenders—" "Of course I remember, " he said. "Of course."

The precise way he spoke surprised her. "I'm sorry," she said, "I didn't—" "That's okay," he said. The tension in his face stiffened his eyebrows. "Go on," he said. "I didn't mean to snap."

She looked down at her hands. She didn't know what to say. "I was scared," she said, "weren't you?"

He laughed out loud. "No," he said. "I wasn't at all scared. Not at all." His eyes focused sharply on her, as if he were reading something in her face. "How old are you?" he said. "Sixteen," she said, "old enough to drive, I guess." She didn't mean it as a joke, but it came out that way. "I mean, old enough to drive a car and not ride a plane." She hoped he would smile, but he didn't. It seemed as if he couldn't smile.

"I have a nineteen-year-old daughter," he said. "Nineteen, I believe—maybe twenty, maybe more."

Marnee imagined a rich girl in a car, a convertible Porsche. "Of course, I don't see her anymore, not often anyway. She doesn't choose to see me either, and she doesn't have to." His stiffness had no fear in it, really. "Perhaps I should go to see her—Emily, that's her name. It might be good for both of us."

"I'm sure it would," Marnee said. "I haven't seen my parents for two whole months, and I'm dying to get home."

"You almost did," he said, nodding at the way she'd said it. He pulled himself up in the chair. "So tell me, dear, do you love your parents?" he said. His eyes tightened.

"Of course," she said. "I've always loved them."

"Someday you'll lose them, you know. It will happen."

He seemed so smart, the way he spoke, the way he looked at her.

"I won't," she said. "Never."

"Of course you will," the man said. "Don't be foolish."

She could have told him everything just then—how they were all Christians and how she knew now that Christ had conquered death. She could have told him, but she waited.

"I buried my father last week," he said. "I'm just now returning home. He was in a facility—a very good one, very expensive. And now he's dead. My father is gone."

"I'm sorry," she said. "I'm sure—"

"You needn't be," he told her. "Death is all there is."

She prayed that God would give her words to speak to him.

....

All around us, Lord, people are hurting. Keep us safe from thinking only about ourselves. Help us to bring Kleenex and comfort to those who need us, whoever they are. In Christ's name may we bring the joy of living in you. Amen.

BLOOD

....
Leviticus 8:14-21

I'm not sure I could have made it in Old Testament times. Blood—vats full of it—ooze from that book. There's more blood in the Old Testament than you'll find in a dozen *Rambo* movies, and that's without the sacrifices. Every time you turn around, a high priest is fileting some ox or sheep or goat (something animal), and blood is flowing—thick and red—all over the place.

Isaac Watts might have been thinking of the kind of ritual you read about in today's Scripture passage when he wrote the second stanza of this hymn, in which he says that God's name will rise, as sweet as perfume from our "every morning sacrifice."

Put yourself back in the Old Testament. You're up at the usual time, just after eight. Before your mom leaves for work she reminds you, for the umpteenth time, to do your morning sacrifice. You yawn and check the cupboards for Lucky Charms.

You eat breakfast, reading the back of the cereal box just as you do every morning, then head outside to the chicken-wire cage where you keep your sacrificial lambs. When you reach the cage, you pause a moment to select an animal. Then you grab the knife and the lamb, pull back it's head, and whoosh!

Ugly. Now I *know* I couldn't make it in the Old Testament!

But it's important to remember what it was all about. All that Old Testament blood—those thousands of morning sacrifices—were God-commanded forms of worship. Blood, in the old rituals, was quite simply life, and when it was let from an animal, it represented life given for others. The blood of butchered lambs became a means by which the Israelites saw themselves cleansed of their sin.

I'm thankful I live in New Testament times. No animal's blood has ever been shed for me, but I'm clean just the same, and I don't have to do morning sacrifices. My sins are gone, washed away by the blood of the Lamb of God—Jesus Christ. Because he lives, no one sacrifices sheep—or goats or oxen.

So, what kind of action is Mr. Isaac Watts talking about when he says "our morning sacrifices"? He's not talking about slaughter. He's talking about giving—sacrificing ourselves.

Our morning sacrifices are our devotions with God; but even more than that, they are the gift of our whole lives to his praise. Our morning sacrifice is our dedication to do God's work. Nothing more—and nothing less. He wants all our days.

The sacrifice you demand of us is our lives, Lord. Help us give you the praise you want by devoting ourselves to doing your work in the world you've created. In Jesus' name, Amen.

INJUSTICE

....
Micah 3:5-12

When Aaron left for the strawberry fields just outside of town, it seemed so early that he was surprised to see that his brother Steve was already back from doing his paper route.

Aaron was twelve, and it was the first summer he was old enough to pick. The grass shone with dew, and the mountains stood like peaceful neighbors in an almost invisible sky, perfectly clear.

Aaron worked all day that first day—from the moment the boss handed out pails right up to quitting time. Sometimes he'd rest for just a minute and scoop up one or two of the best berries, but mostly he picked—even when Steve was chucking clods.

When the pail was full, Aaron would carry it up the row and dump it onto the flats, where a kid weighed up his totals and punched his card. All day he dreamed of the holes in his card, multiplying eleven cents times sixty pounds, then eighty, then a hundred.

The rains never came that season, so Aaron worked every day— even though it wasn't much fun, even though sometimes he wished he could just take a morning off and relax at the pool. Whenever his knees would stiffen or his fingers would burn, he'd think about that check.

After berry season ended, a week passed before the envelope with the window in it made it into their mailbox. At first, Aaron didn't want to open it. He just wanted to hold it in his hand like an unopened treasure. But he had to open it.

When he did, he was disappointed. The total was wrong.

He'd picked 1678 pounds, just like the check said, but the amount was $151.02, less than he'd thought. Steve had beaten him, of course, racked up more than $200. But something wasn't right.

His mother told him he should ask down at the factory, try to figure out why he didn't get what he thought he would. So he did. A man in a Mariners cap said that twelve-year-olds got nine cents a pound this year—not eleven. They got two cents a pound less just because they were twelve.

Aaron didn't know what to say. He had more money than he'd ever seen in his life, but something seemed wrong. The berries he'd picked were worth just as much to the company as the ones Steve had picked. It didn't seem right that Aaron should get two whole cents less per pound.

What made Aaron angry was injustice. Verse four of "Jesus Shall Reign" is about injustice, too, or the lack of it. Isaac Watts claims that wherever Jesus is Lord of the strawberry fields, nobody's going to get taken like Aaron did. No one will get shafted because of their age or their race or their sex. "All who suffer want" are blest in a society where God Almighty is honored, this hymn says.

But is a society's level of wealth an indication of God reigning there? No, no more than Steve's additional cash meant that somehow God favored him. The point of the verse is not that rich nations must— because they are rich—be honoring God. The point is simply this: if you love God, you'll be fair.

Where God comes first, love grows, justice flourishes, joy leaps— and people like Aaron don't get taken.

And God knows. He's the one pouring the blessings.

"Blessings abound where'er he reigns."

Lord, help us to see injustice and to work for those who suffer, for whatever reason. We know that when you are in our hearts, we will help others. Give us the courage to do what is right from day to day.
Amen.

PECULIAR HONORS

....
Psalm 72

I saw him first, and when I did, instinct told me to save my kids. He came in through the dining room, made a couple of eerie turns in perfect silence above my mother's head, then, twitching his wings once or twice, left the room as quietly as he'd entered. I told my kids to scatter—quick.

I don't think I'd ever seen a bat before. I know I'd never seen one in a house. And the eerie sight of one of those furry urchins fluttering its bony wings in our kitchen—right above my kids' hair—turned me into a killer.

I've hit my share of home runs in my life. Right now, I'm batting over .700 on the church slow-pitch team. But I might just as easily have talked the Niagara Falls into flowing uphill as nail a bat with a broom. Their magic sonar keeps them from all kinds of disaster. Just when you think you're going for the long ball, they turn on a dime. I've hit screwballs and big, bad curves, drops and sliders, and even a knuckler or two. But I never touched that lousy bat. No way.

Finally, he disappeared. We looked everywhere until I found that scrawny beast hanging upside down on a curtain. We got a laundry basket from the basement and trapped him against the window, then hauled him outside. He chirped and screamed for awhile, trapped as he was, then wiggled and squirmed until he wrestled himself out of the basket.

Here's the ugly part. When my dad saw him about to take off, he kicked him down, then stomped on him, right in front of the whole family. Seeing him dead brought great relief.

Some of you are thinking that my father did a rotten thing, but I know that if I'd had the nerve, I'd have stomped on that pest myself. Bats make lousy house guests. They don't know when to leave.

After having a bat in the house, it's hard for me to believe, as this hymn says, that every creature should bring "highest" honor to God. Everything, maybe, except bats.

But I know the idea is true—that everything in creation has its use and brings praise. Bats kill insects. According to the latest estimates, in an average year in most parts of North America, there are approximately 41,000 mosquitoes per human being. Without bats, think of the odds. I guess bats have purpose and bring praise.

Each of us—bat and human being alike—brings honors to God. What a bat brings is not what a peacock brings. What you bring may not be what I bring. I suppose this very reading is my form of praise—but so is my teaching, my being a father and a husband, even my being a slow-pitch softball player. Like every other person and creature, I bring my own special honors to my King.

A politician might bring his voting record. An artist might bring her canvas or her bassoon, and a gymnast his trophies. A mom might bring a pailful of dirty diapers, a hog farmer his sows.

In everything we are and do, the song suggests, we bring praise. Every creature—even bats—brings the God of creation gifts of praise: squirrels, monkeys, and hairy-nosed wombats; Africans, Americans, Asians, Europeans, Australians. We're all part of his world. Praise him!

We are all your children, Lord, even if no two of us are exactly the same. May each of us, this day, bring our own peculiar honors to you. May we devote our gifts to your praise. Amen.

OH, FOR A THOUSAND TONGUES TO SING

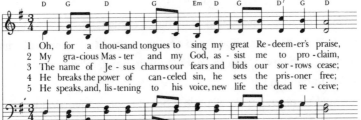

1 Oh, for a thou-sand tongues to sing my great Re-deem-er's praise,
2 My gra-cious Mas - ter and my God, as - sist me to pro - claim,
3 The name of Je - sus charms our fears and bids our sor - rows cease;
4 He breaks the power of can - celed sin, he sets the pris-oner free;
5 He speaks, and, lis - tening to his voice, new life the dead re - ceive;

the glo - ries of my God and King, the tri-umphs of his grace!
to spread through all the earth a - broad the hon - ors of your name.
'tis mu - sic in the sin - ner's ears, 'tis life and health and peace.
his blood can make the foul - est clean; his blood a - vails for me.
the mourn - ful, bro - ken hearts re - joice; the hum - ble poor be - lieve.

6 Hear him, you deaf; you voiceless ones,
　your loosened tongues employ;
　you blind, behold your Savior come;
　and leap, you lame, for joy!

7 To God all glory, praise, and love
　be now and ever given
　by saints below and saints above,
　the church in earth and heaven.

Text: Charles Wesley, 1739, alt.
Tune: Carl G. Gläser, 1828; adapt. and arr. Lowell Mason, 1839

CM
AZMON

CONVERSION

....
John 3:1-5

It would be nice if every one of us had a conversion like Paul's, if God would simply reach down and snatch our sight with some blinding brightness, or if he'd speak to us, bullhorn in hand, telling us which direction to head in life.

It would be great if we'd all have a boom-boom conversion to point back at somewhere in our lives: "Yep, I was on the road to Doon one afternoon, and I've been a new person ever since."

Charles Wesley, experts say, wrote "Oh, For A Thousand Tongues To Sing" on the eleventh anniversary of his conversion— an event that took place when both he and his brother John were around thirty and had already spent a couple years as missionaries. The Wesleys were hardly wild and wicked men. They were *missionaries.* Even when they were in college, other guys chuckled about how methodically the Wesleys lived their lives. In fact, that's where they got their name—the Methodists.

But one day in May of 1738 both John and Charles had some kind of religious experience, a conversion that changed the way they looked at themselves and their faith. Although they'd always been zealous about being Christians, they claimed they'd never personally accepted Jesus Christ nor felt the joy of being Christians. Suddenly, that day, they did.

You can feel conversion celebrated in the hymn. Christ's name, Wesley says in stanzas 3 and 4, charms our fears, bids our sorrows cease, breaks the power of canceled sin, frees prisoners, and cleans the grubbiest among us. That's conversion. You may know kids who've had boom-boom conversions. You may have had one yourself. They happen. Some big conversions rumble down the subterranean faults of some lives like city-splitting earthquakes; some barely bump the Richter scale's needle. But even if our conversions don't exactly shake the timbers, we all have them.

Some day all of us will be able to look back on our lives and point at a time when we first knew God was real. For some of you, that may be happening right now—as it is for Marnee.

Maybe it's the writer in me that says all of you should sit down and think about your lives sometime, put together a story that leads you to the point you're at today—even if you talk about that story only with yourself and tell it to the bedroom ceiling.

This is a conversion hymn. I think any believer can sing it with the Wesley brothers or any other of the millions of people who've been singing it for two hundred and fifty years. It makes no difference if Christ threw your moped off the road one night and beat some sense into you, or if one day you simply felt a prayer push past the ceiling you'd always considered a barrier between you and God.

Conversion, I believe, happens when we know and believe that God, who is very real, loves us enough to have given up his only Son. Knowing that, believing that, sets all of us free.

You've never been converted, you say? Do you know there is a God who loves you? Then you're there. Period.

Dear Lord, help us know you're real. In times when
we doubt, keep us close. Help us always to come to
you and talk. Bring us close when we wander off.
Please, Lord, be our God. Amen.

EXCUSABLE WHITE LIES

....
Psalm 149

I once saw a calf with two heads, but I've never seen a man with a thousand tongues. What's more, I'm not sure I'd want to. Where on earth would he keep them?

Charles Wesley isn't really wishing for a thousand tongues either. What he's doing is playing around with a kind of expression called *hyperbole* or *overstatement*, a white lie that's excusable because, although it's an exaggeration, it's offered in the cause of truth.

You come in one afternoon after painting the deck, and you tell your mother or father that you're starved. You aren't, of course. You're exaggerating to make a point.

"My word, on the Fourth of July there were a million people on the beach." Sure there were.

Hyperbole is often used in the language of love. "I'll love you 'till the rivers all run dry, my dear." Sure you will. Even Juliet, the most famous of Shakespeare's sweethearts, uses overstatement:

> Give me my Romeo; and, when he shall die,
> Take him and cut him out in little stars,
> And he will make the face of heaven so fine
> That all the world will be in love with night,
> And pay no worship to the garish sun.

Hyperbole, as you can see, is a great way to make your point—vividly. And that's what Wesley wanted to do.

So what's Mr. Wesley's point in wishing for a thousand tongues? You might think of it this way. He wishes that his voice would be more like the Mormon Tabernacle Choir. It's awesome to be able to shake chandeliers, rattle windows, and raise the roof. He's simply saying that he wishes he had all the volume in the world to sing God's praise.

But that's not all of it either, I think. Some laboratory genius has discovered that when more than twenty-four voices join together, a kind of grayness begins to appear in the tonal quality of choral music; that is, great masses of people have a tendency to weigh down the harmony with the sheer bulk of their voices, no matter how good they are individually. The sound gets muddied.

Wesley didn't need to be a thousand-voice choir to sing God's praise beautifully. He knew that too. What concerns him in this song about conversion is praise, not his singing voice.

And it seems to me that what he's saying, hyperbolically, is that if he were somehow given one thousand tongues, he would use every last one of them to speak and sing God's praise. He wishes he had more— not so that his own voice would suddenly deepen into the powerful sound of the Mormon Tabernacle Choir, but so that he could praise God a thousand times more than he now can. Think of it this way. If I write for the next twenty years on this computer, I'll probably end up with thousands of pages.

But if I had a thousand pairs of hands and a thousand computers, then I could bring a thousand times more praise to God.

That, it seems to me, is what Charles Wesley, the converted Christian, really means. He's not stretching the truth really.

He's just telling the truth in a way that will make it stick.

Thank you for giving us people like Wesley who can put into words what we feel. Thank you for the thousand tongues of your people. Help us sing with their joy. Amen.

MARNEE'S HOME (8)

....
Psalm 100

The man with sideburns reached in his pocket and pulled out a silver pen. "Here we are," he said, and he drew a circle on a napkin, "and then we die." He crossed it out with an X. "It's like tic-tac-toe—but without the boxes."

"Your father's death must have been very sad," she said.

"Not really," he told her. "Not at all."

"It's hard for me to believe that," she said, but she felt his emptiness. "I'll always love my parents—I'm sure of it."

He giggled a little, and it made her angry.

"Don't laugh at me," she said. "No one likes to be laughed at."

"Perhaps I'm jealous," he said. He pulled himself up from the chair, but didn't walk away. Both hands on his waist, he faced her. "I sat at my father's bedside, and I watched him die—" He stopped. "I don't know why I'm telling you this," he said, pursing his lips, always searching her face.

"His mind had been gone already for eight years, and I wanted him to die. But when he lay there suffering, and when I saw that the nurses didn't care at all for an old man with no reason to live—" He stopped and turned away, took a breath. "I was the only one who cared about my father, the only soul in the world, and when it's my turn, I know I'll be even more alone."

"What about your daughter?" Marnee asked.

"I've done nothing in my life to be a father to her," he said, "nothing at all."

"So you wanted to die on the plane?" she said.

"I would have been happy to go down on that plane," he said. "If you're going to be alone anyway, then why live?"

Marnee felt his pain as he stood before her, looking into the masses of people milling through the gates in the terminal. She asked Christ for words. "I'll pray for you," she said. That's all.

"You'll do what?" he asked, as if he'd misheard.

"I said, 'I'll pray for you.'"

He turned toward her, bringing his hands together at the fingertips. "You'll pray for me?" he asked.

She nodded.

"That's very simple, and that's very dear," he told her, covering his mouth with his fingers. "Thank you," he said. "It means a great deal to me actually." He twisted his head strangely. "How old are you?" he asked.

"Sixteen," she said.

"That's right—I'd already forgotten."

He took her hand like a perfect father and kissed it once.

"No one has ever prayed for me," he said. "No one I know. Thank you so very much," he told her, and then he walked away.

Marnee watched him disappear into the crowd, and she thanked Jesus—he seemed so close—for the simple words. Then she prayed for the rich man with sideburns.

Later that night, Marnee stepped out into the desert heat of Arizona. Her family was there, their faces wrapped in loving smiles. She had so much to tell them. She had so much to say.

Marnee was home.

Thank you for letting us be blessings to other people, Lord. Thank you for helping us to help others, even when that help is only a prayer. In Jesus' name, Amen.

JAILBREAK

....

Isaiah 42:1-7

There's a whole series of good reasons why no convict ever escaped from Alcatraz, an island prison in the middle of San Francisco Bay.

First was the elaborate system of locking the cells. When the prisoners returned after a meal, one key twist locked every cell so that none of them could be opened unless all of them were.

But let's just assume that some Houdini did slide between the bars. The next line of defense were the guards perched above the cell block. Not much could escape their wary eyes.

But let's assume again that someone *did* sneak past—then what? Then he'd have had to get himself outside the building, and considering how heavily bolted Alcatraz's doors and windows were, that would have taken a major miracle.

Okay, let's keep playing: let's assume he gets out. San Francisco's Golden Gate Bridge stands there on the horizon like the open arms of a long-lost love. Just a quick dip in the bay, and boom!—freedom!

Not so fast. If a prisoner dove into that bay, his chances of surviving were dismal. At an almost constant temperature of 55 degrees, the swirling waters would numb him into hypothermia, rendering his whole body useless for the long fight it would take to swim to the city.

So you can see why most people assume that no convict ever escaped Alcatraz successfully. And, as far as I'm concerned, that's all right. Some of them deserved the cooler. Take, for instance, Scarface Capone, the Birdman, Machine Gun Kelley, and Creepy Karpus. Personally, I'd breathe easier knowing those toughs were behind bars.

That's why I've always had trouble with that odd line about prisoners that Wesley included in this hymn: "he sets the prisoners free." I don't like it. And I've often been puzzled about what it means. Surely Christ doesn't think of rapists and thugs as if they were apostles? He's not going to walk into an Alcatraz somewhere, pick out some psycho mass murderer, and set him back out in society, is he? That can't be it.

Perhaps what this line means is that Christ himself frees those prisoners who are *unjustly* imprisoned. Christ's work on earth—and ours as a result—is to bring justice. So Christ picks up and shakes prisoners who shouldn't be in the clink, and softly the chains fall from their ankles and wrists like cheap tin.

But don't forget, this is a song about conversion. The point that Charles Wesley wants us all to celebrate is that even prisoners on death row can be freed by conversion, freed in the very best way there is—from sin and death. That's the miracle.

I wouldn't doubt at all that lots of convicts escaped Alcatraz. They may never have entered the stormy waters of the San Francisco Bay. They may not even have squeezed an inch beyond the guards. But if Christ came into their hearts—even guys with names like Scarface and Machine Gun and Creepy—they escaped. You can bet on it.

We're only free when we're in you, Lord. We're only brave because we know that nothing in this world can separate us from your love. Thank you for being such a comfort, for bringing us such joy beyond fear and beyond prison bars. Amen.

SO FAIR AND FOUL

....
Matthew 20:1-16

Really bad men fascinate me—men like the famous "Scarface" Capone of Chicago. Actually Alphonse "Scarface" Capone was born in Naples, Italy, and grew up tough in Brooklyn, New York. But he made his name in Chicago during those years when laws against drinking drove the liquor industry into the hands of the mob—the hands of thugs like Capone.

On February 14, 1929, Capone's men, dressed up like cops, machine-gunned seven men against a brick wall in one of Chicago's bloodiest murders ever. Capone never got caught. By 1927 he was worth 100 million. After the government landed him in jail on tax evasion, he spent eight years in prison, then died of syphilis.

"His blood can make the foulest clean" we say when we turn to "Oh, for a Thousand Tongues to Sing." Do you think someday in heaven you'll run into Scarface?

The truth is, you could. What happened between Capone and God in the last moments of his life could have been enough. We may not like to hear that, but it's true—the foulest clean.

Most of us have trouble picturing bad or ugly people in heaven— people like Capone or people like Sherburn. . .

Everyone knows Sherburn is a geek—even he does. He wears his top button closed all the time, let's his hair grow untouched over his ears like a thatched roof, and peppers his lips with blue spots by sucking on his Bic. Above all, he stinks. Sherburn, his name is. He's sixteen, and he goes home after school and plays with Legos.

Sherburn goes to your church. Yech. He goes to your Bible camp. Double yech. He's in your youth group. Triple yech.

Sherburn's a Christian.

Inside, you wish he weren't. Inside, you wish the only kids in your youth group were the athletes and the "with-its." Not the Sherburns. Yech.

We might not like it, but God loves the bad—and the ugly.

Tell you what, let's try another character—a character most of us would admire.

Benj started at forward when he was a sophomore and led his basketball team in rebounds. He's got a screaming Ninja—goes from zero to sixty in six seconds. When Benj lifeguards, he picks up a perfect tan, color-coordinated with his bronzed hair. He's a hunk.

Inside, he knows it. To Benj, kids like Sherburn are dead, invisible.

Benj is the president of your youth group—even though he ignores Sherburn and other members who don't come up to his standards. He's the most popular boy in your church, your school, maybe even your whole town.

The good (-looking), the bad, and the ugly. They could all be God's own people—even though they're so different—because his blood can make the foulest clean, even the ones who don't look at all grungy—even the fairest of the foul.

Sometimes I wish God would let me choose his people. I know who I'd pick—mostly people like Benj. We could make this whole Christianity business into something really popular. Kids would be streaming in.

But that's not God's way. "That one over there," he says, "the one with the holes in her pants—that one's mine. And that kid with the black eye. Oh yeah, that cocky one over there too. They're all mine." And then he smiles, this God of ours.

Maybe it seems unfair to us that some horrible sinners could be saved, Lord, but we know it's true. Your grace isn't always easy for us to understand. You've saved us too. You've chosen us for no reason we can understand. We praise you, our God. Help us live in thankfulness for what you've done. Amen.

ABIDE WITH ME

1 A - bide with me: fast falls the e - ven - tide;
2 Swift to its close ebbs out life's lit - tle day;
3 I need your pres - ence ev - ery pass - ing hour.
4 I fear no foe with you at hand to bless,
5 Hold now your Word be - fore my clos - ing eyes.

the dark - ness deep - ens; Lord, with me a - bide.
earth's joys grow dim, its glo - ries pass a - way.
▸ What but your grace can foil the tempt - er's power?
though ills have weight, and tears their bit - ter - ness.
Shine through the gloom and point me to the skies.

When oth - er help - ers fail and com - forts flee
Change and de - cay in all a - round I see.
▸ Who like your - self my guide and strength can be?
Where is death's sting? Where, grave, your vic - to - ry?
Heaven's morn - ing breaks and earth's vain shad - ows flee;

Help of the help - less, O a - bide with me.
O Lord who chang - es not, a - bide with me.
▸ Through cloud and sun - shine, O a - bide with me.
I tri - umph still, if you a - bide with me.
in life, in death, O Lord, a - bide with me.

Text: Henry F. Lyte, 1847, alt.
Tune: William H. Monk, 1861

10 10 10 10
EVENTIDE

"HIS BLOOD CAN MAKE THE FOULEST CLEAN"

LONELINESS

....
Psalm 139:1-12

Carol, 37, has been married for fifteen years to Eddie, a man she settled for because he didn't seem dangerous and because he promised to help her escape from the faceless voices in the dictating machine she had listened to for too many forty-hour weeks. If ever love existed between Carol and Eddie, it was swept away long ago by the wave of silence that envelops the couple and never seems to break. The couple's two children, both in junior high, don't seem to need Carol anymore. No one does. The family lives in emptiness on a street full of houses full of people that Carol doesn't know.

▼

Rushton Elementary is so small that the fifth and sixth grades sit together in one room and still total only twenty-three kids. Eleven are boys, Bruce among them, and they all love sports. All except Bruce. Bruce not only dislikes sports but also isn't any good at them—right-handed or left-handed. So every night after school Bruce goes home alone. The guys out playing ball on the diamond don't even see him kicking stones along the street, his head down.

▼

When Frank's wife, Evelyn, died, it came as no surprise. She'd been sick since the day she'd gone alone up to bed rather than tell him how tired she felt. What surprised Frank was how everything in the house spoke once Evelyn was gone, as if some memory of the years they'd spent together were planted in every cup and every saucer and awaited only his touch. The light at the top of the stairs, the orange-juice pitcher, the stains around the dial of the phone—all of it spoke of Evelyn.

▼

This hymn, "Abide with Me," is about loneliness. Whether people are old or young, married or single, rich or poor, black or white, they can suffer loneliness. Go to Nevada's desert mountains or Toronto's busiest streets, and you'll find loneliness. It grows everywhere.

I probably don't need to argue that the loneliest time in our lives is that time when we die. In an old medieval play titled *Everyman*, the main character nearly goes crazy trying to get someone to come along with him to his death. Of course, no one does. And the character can't understand why. What are friends for, he wonders?

Perhaps Henry Francis Lyte sensed the loneliness of dying as he finished writing a poem he'd begun years earlier. The story goes that he'd heard a dying man repeat the phrase "Abide with me," as if it were a prayer. He'd written that phrase down somewhere, then started a poem.

Almost twenty-five years later, suffering from both asthma and tuberculosis, Lyte resigned his ministry at the oceanside village of Lower Brixham, Devonshire, England. A doctor had told him the only way he could recover his strength would be by leaving the clammy cold for a warmer, dryer climate. While clearing out his desk, Lyte found the poem he'd started, spent some time in the garden working it through, then finished it.

It was September, 1847, when Lyte finished "Abide with Me," and he may well have known that he was, already then, on that lonely road to his own death. He died on November 20 of that same year.

No friends come along on the trip to the graveyard. Your only companion on the most lonely walk of your life is God. When there is no one else, he is there, always, through cloud and sunshine. With Christ, we are never alone.

....

We can be in the middle of hundreds of people on a street somewhere, Lord, and feel as if we are the only people on the face of the earth. But you are always with us—in the middle of the wilderness and in the jungle of the city. You've given us your Spirit, Lord. Thank you. Amen.

CHANGE AND DECAY

....

Malachi 3:1-6

Nestled in the mountains near Camp Verde, Arizona, is what's left of Jerome, Arizona—a city once built around a big silver mine. Many people call Jerome a ghost town, but some folks still call it home.

Most of the city is falling apart, from the rows of big Victorian houses to the ramshackle remains of miners' cabins shoehorned into the steep sides of the hill.

Once I met a man who lives in Jerome. He told me that the town didn't know what to do about the mess. More and more tourists were stopping up at the old mining city and walking down its deserted streets as if it were an outdoor museum. He said the city was trying to decide whether to fix up the homes.

"But if you do, this place won't look like a ghost town," I told him. "Why can't you just let it stay the way it is?" "Because the houses *won't* stay this way," he said. "They'll keep rotting until nothing's left. Then what'll we have?"

Things decay, this hymn says. Abandoned, Jerome would simply disintegrate. Doors would continue to fall off, porch steps would curl, floorboards would warp between the soaking rains and hot desert sun. Things would just get worse and worse and worse.

In time, all things decay: guitars warp, gardens get weedy, motors run tight, knees stiffen, hamburger spoils, computer discs lose their charge, faces wrinkle, jeans shrink, buttons fall off, bellies sag, and Coke loses its zing. The father of a friend of mine once told her, "You're spreading out like a thirty-dollar cow." He said it as a joke. But people do spread out, like it or not.

Alice Cooper, a punk rocker from way back, once offered this view of history: "Things just get worse and worse and worse." Doesn't that sound wonderful?

I'm not sure he's right. Some things get better with time—like wine and violins and love. If I still had a Henry Aaron baseball card from 1958, I could make some money. Coins and stamps get more valuable. So do Thunderbirds and toy tractors.

A couple years ago the Des Moines, Iowa, public school system decided to put the walls back in between the toilets in the city high schools. They'd been taken out several years before to help administrators police the drug deals. But kids aren't using drugs like they used to in Des Moines. Things are getting better. Drug use is down.

Is the hymn wrong, then? Is life getting better instead of worse?

That question doesn't have a clean answer. Some things are getting better—sure. But change and decay continue to surround us. For example, when people get older—and I'm including myself here, folks—they tend to look back longingly on the "good old days." Ahhh, yes.

This is a song about sadness and loneliness, and seeing the end. It's not a song about the joy of the Christian life or the overflowing power of the Holy Spirit. It's simply about God's being there, always, for better or for worse, through growth and decay. What a friend we have in Jesus—that's its theme.

He is. He will be. Your gutters might leak and your roof may need some help, but with Christ you'll never stand alone.

Dear Lord, sometimes it seems as if our whole world is going down the tubes. Help us to see your hand in our lives and in the world itself. Help us to know that you're in charge. Amen.

THE ARCH-FIEND

....

1 John 4:1-7

Ten years ago, maybe more, a TV comedian named Flip Wilson pulled a kind of miracle by making *Satan* a household word. In fact, the line he repeated, week after week, became one of those famous TV ditties like "Well, excu-u-u-use me!" or "Isn't that just spaaa-cial?"

If I'm not mistaken, he delivered his pet line while he was playing a bossy old woman, a woman who took great pride in her own fussy Christianity. Whenever he (she) would do something bad, the line would bob up like an excuse: "Oooohhh, the devil made me do it." The crowd would roar, then take the line home and use it for laughs every chance they got. Flip's little saying became very in.

Of course, Flip Wilson wasn't the first to use that line. He was quoting someone far better known. Original credit for that line goes, of course, to Eve—Adam's sweetheart. When God asked her to explain why she and Adam were hiding from him, Eve said that eating the apple wasn't her fault because the devil made her do it.

She, of course, was only following her husband's lead. He didn't blame the snake; he blamed her. They both blamed someone else. Their sin couldn't have been their fault—not such good people. The devil made them do it.

The real devil probably chuckles when he hears people repeat that excuse. Flip Wilson's popular ditty made Satan silly. What's silly can't be serious. Thus, Flip's flippant line made Satan into somebody with the power and reputation, say, of Goofy.

Now you and I may not enjoy being laughed at—at least I don't. But Satan, who's not in the least human, does. If we take Satan as seriously as we do Porky Pig, then it's a whole lot easier for him to burrow into us and do his work.

Jason thought Mike was his friend until one day when Mike took off with some other guys and yelled something at Jason, as if Jason were dirt. Jason boiled. That day, Jason saw Mike's bike at school. When no one was looking, he kicked his foot through the spokes. The principal caught him. "How come?" he asked. Jason looked down at his hands. "I guess the devil got into me," he said.

Is Jason right? In a way. When he was standing there looking at that bike, he wasn't listening to God's voice. He listened instead to Satan's prompting, telling him that nothing tasted quite as sweet as revenge.

But does that excuse him? Obviously not. Did it excuse Eve for picking the apple? Nope. When she bit into the apple and gave it to her husband, sin came into the world through their disobedience. They were punished.

The old pictures of Satan—the horned monster draped in blood red or midnight black, with a pointed tail that swings out, snake-like, from his behind—may be a little silly, just as silly as Flip's Wilson's humor. But the devil is no cartoon. He's alive and kicking and living in all of our hearts.

Listen to what John says: "The one who is in you [God] is greater than the one who is in the world [Satan]" (1 John 4:4). Only God makes Satan silly.

You can make the devil into a silly joker, Lord. Give us confidence and grace to fight evil and to be your people in the world you've made. Amen.

LIFE AND DEATH IN THE FAMILY

....
Romans 8:38-39

About a year ago a silver-haired gentleman wearing a goatee rang our back doorbell at about eight in the morning—the time of day, especially during the school year, when we're much too busy to be very pleasant. But it was soon apparent he didn't come to visit *us*. He came to visit our house.

"I spent my entire childhood in this house," he said, as if I weren't even there. He pointed at the family room, at the corner where our television stands. "I was born right there in that room," he told me.

To think that birth took place right in the room where my kids watch cartoons is a little strange. But years ago most kids, I'm told, were born at home. The older kids were quickly shooed out of the way, so a birth wasn't really a public event. But most kids bawled out their first breaths in their own homes instead of in the shiny (and safe!) hospital maternity ward.

Death, too, at one time took place more frequently at home than it does today. It's unlikely that death occured while an entire family stood around and drank tea, but when someone died right in the house, right there among the family members, death itself—the event—may well have seemed less of a stranger than it does to some of us today.

It's fair to say that Elizabeth Kubler-Ross's book, *On Death and Dying*, changed the way all of us think about death— especially those deaths that occur after long bouts with disease and injury. Kubler-Ross claims that by locking death up behind hospital doors, we are hurting ourselves as well as the dying person. When death occurs only in a hospital room, we have a hard time thinking of death as something natural—a part of life. That, she says, hurts us.

She claims we not only hurt ourselves but also the people who are dying by sticking them in hospitals. We make dying difficult when we shut someone up in an oxygen tent and string him up with beeping and flashing lights. Being in one's own home, claims Kubler-Ross, allows a person to feel more comfortable with dying.

Kubler-Ross and others helped create the idea of the *hospice.* Maybe you've never heard of the word before. A hospice is not exactly a hospital and not exactly a home. It's a place where terminally ill people spend their last weeks, a place they can decorate to make themselves feel comfortable—to make them feel more like people than patients. Hospices are found, today, almost all over North America.

The speaker of "Abide with Me" asks God to hold the Word high so that in his dying "gloom" he can keep his eyes on God's promises and find peace in the victory that Christ's death and resurrection give to his people. He asks God to make spiritual hospice, to make him feel comfortable as he walks down that last lonely path.

Let's get something straight. Dying at home isn't going to take a bite out of death's power. No family pictures, no room full of relatives, no favorite music is going to stop death.

Only Christ does that. That's comfort—all through life.

Our only comfort in dying is knowing that we belong to you. Our only real comfort in living is the same knowledge. You are our Savior and friend, our God, the Ruler of the universe. Amen.